"The first time I read Craig's manusc̲ with excitement! The lessons containe tical and transformational. At several points during that first reading, I was so stirred; I had to lay the manuscript down and pace the floor in prayer! I give this book my strongest possible endorsement! This book has a weightiness that I believe only comes when lessons have been purified by the fires of experience."

—**Jason Benedict**, author, RCE Strategist, MBA; MA, Missiology
Regent University, Center for Entrepreneurship
Virginia Beach, Virginia

"I was so excited to read *Authorized*. We are in a day and an hour of establishing the Kingdom like never before and Jesus gave us the pattern to pray, "Thy Kingdom Come, Thy Will be Done." *Authorized* comes from the heart of an apostle that I personally know and have seen the fruit of the lives and nations Craig Kuehn has touched. This isn't an intellectual treatise or a recital of biblical doctrine. This is battle strategy forged from revelation on the battlefield. Whether you are a minister, a business person, a parent or simply a member of society, this book will be effective in teaching and activating you in Apostolic, Governmental, Kingdom Prayer."

—**Dr. Kathy Tolleson**, international author,
speaker, and spiritual counselor
Kingdom Life Now, Inc.
Daytona Beach, Florida

"It is rare that I have an opportunity to recommend an author who has such insight, revelation and integrity. Craig Kuehn is not just speaking from head knowledge, but experiential knowledge. I have been with him in the nations of the earth and seen his leadership change culture and the lives of people. Please read this book carefully because it has the potential of renewing your vision and molding your life into the image of Christ."

—**Bishop Paul D. Zink**, author,
founder of New Life Christian Fellowship,
and founder of Providence School of Jacksonville, Inc.
Jacksonville, Florida

"Having a mutual passion for missions, and knowing Craig for many years, I was delighted to share the reading of this manuscript with my wife. As we delved into the heart of Craig's work, we encountered a "line upon line, precept upon precept" awakening that was a clarion call for accessing a newfound plane of authority in prayer. God's wonderful surprise to us was that Craig gave written understanding to what God had recently begun orchestrating in our own lives. He has been divinely endowed with a specific message, that if acted upon in faith and expectation, will literally change the course of your life and those you stand between heaven and earth for. We highly recommend not only reading this book but studying the biblically based teachings and activating the authoritative prayers in your life and ministry."

—**Rod and Celeste Groomer**, former executive leader and Director of the Global Mission Major at Christ For The Nations Institute, advisors to the Board of Directors at Christ For The Nations Institute, and founders of Geobound Mission Ministry
Dallas, Texas

"This book written by Craig Kuehn is not from theory but practice. I've seen Craig minister in the field, and his vision for reaching other nations and always going to the next level is inspiring. Craig has lived out the reality of these principles. God has unfolded the truth of praying out the Word under the inspiration of the Holy Spirit and watching the results unfold. Nations have been opened up through this prophetic praying and it has been a door opener for their ministry. The truths gleaned from this book are vital for the hour in which we live. We need to exercise and step out in these revelations, push back the darkness and open up the doors of opportunity for the gospel to spread in this last and final hour of our age. Insightful. Powerful. Needed. Doable. Wonderful."

—**Pastor Mirek Hufton**, author, international speaker, and Founding Pastor and Senior Pastor of World Harvest Church Roswell, Georgia

AUTHORIZED

UTHORIZED

ESSENTIAL
PRAYER STRATEGIES
FOR AN
UNPRECEDENTED HOUR

CRAIG KUEHN

An Imprint of Go To Nations
Jacksonville, Florida 32207

ISBN-13: 978-0-9967052-5-7
ISBN-10: 09967052-5-2

Library of Congress Control Number: 2017942129

Printed in the United States of America

Cover Design: Craig Kuehn and Tim Dahn, www.timdahn.com

Published by Go To Nations Publishing
3771 Spring Park Road
Jacksonville, Florida 32207

DEDICATION

To my mother, Shirley (now eighty-one), and my grandmother, Thelma, who is awaiting the rest of us in Heaven. I feel very much like Timothy in the New Testament, whose mother and grandmother taught him Scripture from an early age. Being the son and grandson of women who know how to pray and have prayed every day of my entire life clears the way for God to do great things. Thank you for the generational pass.

To my wife and partner for life, Sandra. This is our forty-second year of marriage, and it has been a divine partnership from the beginning. Neither I nor Asia would be what we are today without her servant heart, wisdom, unconditional love, and sacrificial example. I may have written a book, but Sandra lives one every day. Thank you for never giving up on anyone.

To the Holy Spirit, who reveals truth found in these pages in practice, Scripture, and revelation. He is constantly calling me to places in Christ I never dreamed of going. Most of the work I have done in this season is a result of the Holy Spirit waking me in the middle of the night with a lot to say. I would like to say that He wrote this book and not me, but since He does work through an imperfect and "in process" creation, I may have gotten in His way a couple of times. But without His inspiration and impartation, this book would not exist.

CONTENTS

FOREWORD

Through his book *Authorized*, Rev. Craig Kuehn has placed mighty tools—prayers of declaration—into our hands that will put us on the offensive. We are challenged to take up arms and to report for duty as soldiers and watchmen on the wall. As a veteran minister of the Gospel and an apostolic father to nations around the world, Craig shares his personal journey on how God led him into a deeper understanding of spiritual identity that has helped thousands of believers to walk in the fullness of their inheritance as true sons of God.

As you read this book, Reverend Kuehn systematically prepares you for war. Each chapter helps to spiritually align your prayer life in a way that will properly position you to be an effective instrument of God to release His will in this present age.

If there is one central message that the Holy Spirit is trying to convey to the Church in this hour, it would be this—it is time to grow up! We are living in a time when it is essential for believers in Christ to know how to navigate in prayer in a way that it shifts the spiritual climate, causing spiritual, physical, and social change around us. God is challenging us to move beyond our day-to-day maintenance-type prayers and become a conduit that releases His will from Heaven into the earth (Matt. 6:10).

God will not go over the head of His Church to do things in spite of our actions or the lack thereof. This would abort His plan to bring us to full maturity in the Son. Through Jesus Christ, the work on Calvary destroyed Satan's authority and canceled all of his claims. God placed the enforcement of Calvary's victory in our hands (Matt. 18:18; Luke 10:17–19).

As born-again believers in Christ, God has given to us "power of attorney" and made us His deputies. But this delegated authority is wholly inoperative apart from Holy Spirit-empowered prayers of a believing Church. Prayer, therefore, is where the action is. It is God's intention that the Church militant should walk in the same life, power, and divine liberty as Jesus did.

In 2 Corinthians 10:4–5 (TLB), the Apostle Paul exhorts us with these encouraging words: "I use God's mighty weapons, not those made by man, to knock down the devil's strongholds. These weapons can break down every proud argument against God and every wall that can be built to keep men from finding Him. With these weapons, I can capture rebels and bring them back to God, and change them into men whose hearts' desire is obedience to Christ."

In Matthew 5:13–14, Jesus reveals a sobering revelation about His Church with these words: "You are the salt of the earth…You are the light of the world." These are not words to be taken lightly. At this present moment, the Church, in union with her risen and enthroned Lord, is the fundamental preserving factor in this present world order. Therefore, by virtue of our organic relationship with Christ, we (not Satan) hold the balance of power in human affairs.

It has been said, "The fate of the world is in the hands of nameless saints." This truth is wonderfully set forth in Psalm 149:5–9: "Let the saints be joyful in glory: let them sing aloud upon their beds. Let the high praises of God be in their mouth, and a two-edged sword in their hand; To execute vengeance upon the heathen, and punishments upon the people; To bind their kings with chains, and their nobles with fetters of iron; To execute upon them the judgment written: this honour have all his saints. Praise ye the Lord."

What makes the book, *Authorized*, so useful for all believers are the powerful, laid-out prayers of declaration that Reverend Kuehn wrote under the leading of the Holy Spirit. Now you can be one of God's

prayer warriors by coming into agreement with Scripture as you make these biblical declarations over your family, church, nation, and the world.

No longer count yourself as insignificant to God's plans or helpless when it comes to the present social and spiritual deterioration we are witnessing in our nations. You were put on this earth to be a gatekeeper—a difference-maker. God made you a force for civilization and enlightened social consciousness. *Authorized* will empower you to take your position in the body of Christ and be a voice that drives back darkness and brings truth, healing, deliverance, freedom, and newness of life to those who are bound. This is the purpose for which you were created!

Dr. Jerry Williamson
President, Go To Nations

ACKNOWLEDGMENTS

I must acknowledge the President of Go To Nations, Dr. Jerry Williamson, and our Executive Vice President of Global Ministries, Nancy Lovelace, for their spiritual leadership and example in prayer. For the last twenty-seven years, I have worked for and with leaders who pray and never settle. Jerry and Nancy carry true apostolic mandates and wield their mantles tirelessly and effectively with global impact. Nancy deserves some of the credit for insisting that the prayers we were praying become something we could pass on to others and for exercising her deeply honed gifts to pull it out of me and see it come to life.

I also want to thank our Executive Vice President of Mobilization, Sandra Barfield. I have known and worked with Sandra for almost twenty years. Sandra is dedicated and passionate about the cause of Christ. As soon as

it hit her inbox, she took it as a personal mission to see it published with excellence and has not relented.

I want to thank Vanessa Sambrano, our first millennial Vice President (of Equipping), and a welcomed voice from and for her generation. She carries what we carry for the nations, but it comes in her package and not ours, which is refreshing. Vanessa did a lot of prework on this book to help us find the right path forward.

My sincere appreciation goes to Deborah Barnes for her many hours of proofing and editing. Deborah wears many hats at Go To Nations: she is the Director of Global Prayer, a Member Care Team member, and writer and editor. I wanted her to read the book because of her spiritual insight and am grateful that her eyes include grammatical insight as well.

Finally, my heartfelt gratitude to Michelle Mauricio for shouldering the unenviable task of taking everyone's changes, ideas, and suggestions and doing the final edit. Michelle spent countless hours working back and forth with each of us to proof, polish, and get this book ready to print.

It is indeed an honor to work with Go To Nations, our world headquarters' staff, volunteers, and a global apostolic family that daily spend their lives to see the cause of Christ advance whatever the cost. It is my pleasure to run this race with you all.

INTRODUCTION

The Lord sowed the original seed for this prayer book in the mid-1990s. As the ministry was growing in Southeast Asia, we were finding ourselves being invited deeper and deeper into Buddhist, Hindu, Communist, and Muslim nations. These nations are often less than 1 percent Christian, and most had never seen a significant move of God. The oppressive spiritual atmosphere was more than tangible as we ministered and taught where darkness had ruled for thousands of years. Personally, we and several members of our team came under spiritual attack. We fought debilitating sickness, had some near-death experiences, and would see sudden ambushes and accidents. No doubt we were locked in battle.

In one of our morning team prayer meetings, the Lord gave me three words. Each built upon the previous word. The first word was "expectation," meaning we needed to raise the level of what we were truly expecting from our heavenly Father in both prayer and practice. God was drawing me deeper and deeper into understanding sonship at the time, and I was seeing that sons, in the Father's business, approached Kingdom life with much more confidence and assurance.

The second word He dropped into my spirit was "declaration." He showed me we were always asking for things He had already promised to give us throughout His Word. In essence, "You don't need to keep asking for what I have already promised you could have." We needed to instead put His Word into action.

The third word I heard was "navigation." As a ministry, we had been working in the nations since 1981. We were not novices, and the New Testament is a pretty good primer on how to advance the Kingdom in unreached places and hostile spiritual environments. But the farther we extended into those places, the more "uncharted" those waters were. While we know the Gospel is the ship that carries us, and the Holy Spirit is the wind who empowers the ship to move, actually navigating those waters requires a divinely inspired strategy each and every time. We knew how to sail—that wasn't the issue; we needed to learn to navigate in new territory.

We had a limited understanding of what that all meant at the time, but we continued to advance in nations and seek God for greater revelation as we did. With each new challenge, we sought and learned new spiritual truth that moved us forward. Over the years, more pieces were added and a greater level of understanding continued to develop, and we saw greater and greater results through our prayers.

As the season changed and I matured, my eyes moved higher and higher from just the day-to-day battles we all face to the strategies, weapons, keys, and Kingdom authority Heaven reveals. This is imperative for us to effectively advance in our own family, our city, our nation, or in any nation on earth.

There are lots of ways to pray in the Bible, all of them correct, depending on what your assignment is, what the strategy of Heaven is for that assignment, and what season you are in. Scripture is clear that we don't get to just make things up, speak them out, and expect Heaven to move. We speak His Word, declaring it to be the final word on every matter, as He directs (Isa. 40:8).

What you now have in your hand are Prayers of Declaration, each drawn directly from Scripture, which I personally, and the entire ministry, have been speaking over our families, our ministry, our government, the nations, and our business partners, all with steadily increasing results.

It all belongs to Him, and He has authorized us, His Church, to claim His rightful inheritance in the nations (Ps. 2:8) or our own cities (Gen. 12:1–3) so that the mountain of the Lord shall be established over all other mountains (Zech. 8:3). Now is the time!

We are seizing this moment from Heaven.

"My heart overflows with a good theme; I address my verses to the King; My tongue is the pen of a ready writer" (Ps. 45:1, NASB).

Craig Kuehn
Vice President of Ministries, Go To Nations
Email: authorizedbook@gotonations.org
Website: www.gotonations.org/kuehn

1

TO HIM WHO HAS

For whoever has, to him more shall be given, and he will have an abundance
—Matthew 13:12, NASB

Several years ago, this was a verse I could not escape. It resonated in my spirit day after day, month after month. God impressed on me, once again, Heaven's intended process for those of us who are in pursuit of spiritual truth.

This verse is repeated almost word for word in Matthew 13, Mark 4, and Luke 8, all in the context of the parable of the sower. The parable of the sower is about seeds of spiritual truth that come to us in various ways, with various challenges, and with varying results. One thing we learn here, and in other Scriptures as well, is that all spiritual truth comes to us in seed form.

Matthew 17:20 says, "Faith starts as a mustard seed."

1 Peter 1:23 says, "We are born again by imperishable seed." The parable of the sower clearly illustrates this principle.

Genesis 8:22 says, "As long as the earth remains, seedtime and harvest… shall not cease."

What we get as truth from God and His Word most often comes as a seed. The key to unlocking impossibilities is what we do with those seeds. That is why each time the parable is repeated in the Gospels this thought is added to bring understanding: "to him who has shall be given more and he shall have in abundance."

You see the process? Have, more, in abundance. That is how Heaven wants truth to work in our lives. When you get something, anything from God, it is a seed. The eternal fruitfulness and **daily** effectiveness of that seed depend on what we do with the seed.

We start with seed, and if we hold it in our hearts, return to it from time to time, recognize a year, two, or five years later that something we are learning enlarges our understanding of the seed we have been carrying, we move from "having truth" to "having more truth." That is how my understanding of authorized governmental prayer has grown.

Spiritual knowledge is "line upon line" and "precept upon precept" as we read in Isaiah 28. How do we learn math? We first just recognize the numbers and what they even mean. Then we learn to move them around, to empower processes such as addition, subtraction, multiplication, and so on. From that, we can do geometry, physics, calculus, and more. We can send a rocket to the moon and bring it home safely—but not without first knowing one plus one equals two.

God does the same thing. The most profound spiritual truth comes at the most rudimentary level. If we overlook it and let it lie dormant, it never becomes more than a basic symbol. But if we apply what we have, and add to it as the years go by, it becomes more—more effective, more efficient, more powerful, and more fruitful, and eventually becomes abundant truth with supernatural results!

Didn't Jesus say He came that we might have abundant life? We go from the **seed** of incorruptible life to **abundant** life by the pursuit of spiritual truth, understanding, knowledge, and application.

This process sets the context for this book. All along the way, I was learning seeds of prayer truth. I was learning that while the truth we receive is indeed that, "a truth" or "some truth," each truth is part of a much bigger spiritual realm of understanding. Jesus is "the Truth," meaning all truth abides in Him, and He is the sum total of all truth. When I receive any truth from God, while it may be full and complete in itself, I must also recognize that with God there is always more to be added to what I know. If I continue to pursue the truth I have been given, at some point in the future an even greater measure or revelation of that truth can be added or unlocked. Unless I pursue the basics of math, I can never master the depths of math—or language or science or anything else.

If that is how the universe works in the natural, why would it be any different in the spiritual? 1 Corinthians 15:46 says just that—the natural comes first and then the spiritual. By bringing me an understanding of the principle of truth in seed form and the process of "have, more, and abundance," I have continued to pursue prayer that truly changes nations, governments, ministries, and destinies.

The current truth in this book is a result of truth upon truth, precept upon precept, obedience upon obedience, advancement upon advancement, practice upon practice, and so on for more than three decades now. In these preliminary chapters, I want to briefly build a biblical "truth" case for authorized prayers at a governmental level. Decrees and declarations that we are seeing have a much deeper impact and much quicker results than anything we have seen in our lifetime.

2

YOUR KINGDOM COME

Our family moved as missionaries to Manila, Philippines, in 1991. In the grand scheme of things, we were pretty unprepared. My wife, Sandra, and I had attended and graduated from Christ for the Nations Institute (CFNI), so we had a proven foundation for launching into ministry. But what we knew and understood about life in another culture, and a spiritual climate much different from our own, was severely lacking. And we were a bit naïve in just how far the devil's schemes and strategies would be unleashed to stop us before we even got started.

But nineteen years later, we were still there, and twenty-seven years later, we are still going strong, touching more nations than ever before. Why? P-R-A-Y-E-R. I knew when we arrived that I didn't know everything I needed to know. CFNI didn't teach me everything. Go To Nations

couldn't teach me everything. My home church and pastor had certainly not taught me how to survive, let alone thrive in the nations. But as the once-blind, now-healed man says in John 9, "one thing I know" I didn't know everything. I didn't know enough, but I knew how to pray. That, above all things, was what we learned in Bible School. Thank you, Christ for the Nations.

Our son Judah was just ten years old when we arrived, and he was sick almost the entire first year. We had some "people challenges" with other missionaries, which threatened our desire to even be on the mission field. When our finances were attacked and we were terribly under budget, I prayed. As I begin to feel the oppression and coercion of the enemy, I began to fast and pray, and pray and fast, and fast and pray. You don't pray "God bless me" prayers and survive in enemy territory.

I knew "the weapons of our warfare are not carnal," and "God always causes us to triumph in Christ Jesus." Those truths were mostly unproven at that point, but I began to apply what I knew in daily, fervent, and scripturally rooted prayer. In that first year, I fasted nearly as much as I ate. I was determined at a faith level that God didn't send us to Asia to let the devil, circumstances, or others take us out. With God's help, we remained steadfast that first year, challenges and all.

By the beginning of the second year, some things had changed on the team. Our greatest "people challenge" at the time was gone, and we had moved into a brand-new little townhouse on the edge of Manila. It felt like a new season, and we were stronger physically and wiser spiritually. Our home was in a small village, or subdivision, that had only two streets merging at a gated entrance. It was new, it was clean, it was safe, so we felt much more at peace and confident.

However, after a few months, we began to feel restless in the night. We didn't hear things or see anything. There were no noises that woke us up, but at all hours of the night, our spirits would become agitated or disturbed. We had no idea what that meant, but we recognized something was out of order in the spirit realm, so I began to pray. What I did not know then was I was praying a "seed truth" prayer that twenty years later would become the foundation for this very book.

I began to pray this one very simple prayer, day after day, week after week, month after month. From the Lord's prayer in Matthew, chapter 6, I began to pray, "Your Kingdom come—Your Kingdom come." I didn't understand that phrase with nearly the understanding I have today, but even then I had enough truth to apply it in faith.

I had done enough, studied enough, and had enough revelation to know that when I said "Kingdom," it meant "government." It meant "rulership." It meant "the reign of the Almighty." I wasn't just throwing words out because Jesus said: "Pray this way." I knew in my spirit that I was in prayer, invoking the supreme rule of God over the situation. I knew it, even though I didn't even know what the situation was.

Suddenly (months later), something happened. It was late in the afternoon, the sun was just setting, and two black SWAT vehicles roared down our street, fully loaded with a brigade of armed and armored men. They literally jumped off the vehicle and immediately flattened the front door of a townhouse about three doors down from us. For nearly two hours, they hauled people and large stone artifacts out of that townhouse. We soon found out those artifacts were imported from China and were filled with illegal drugs. We had a drug den no more than three doors down from us! Drug dealers had been coming and going in the night, and that's why our spirits were restless.

One simple prayer, prayed with understanding, by just one person as far as I know, shut all that down. "Your Kingdom Come" is one of the most powerful prayers in Scripture because it is the government, the rulership of God, that authorizes **all** we do in prayer. Jesus said, "**All** authority is given to me, so I authorize you." That is the foundation of authorized governmental prayer, the prayers in this book.

3

CLAIMING INHERITANCE

By the mid-1990s, I had gone from teaching in the Bible school Go To Nations had established to being the school's director. Sandra and I had led a couple of mission trips with our students into other nations, and I had already seen that our calling was beyond Manila and what we were doing in the Philippines. We were surrounded by the largest and most unreached nations of the world. Two out of three people in the world live on the continent of Asia and are almost entirely unevangelized. This burden was growing and beginning to overwhelm my heart.

The call always comes with opportunities to obey and to follow. Hebrews 11 says, "by faith, Abraham obeyed, when he was called to go to a place he would later receive as an inheritance." I was about to begin a journey toward *biblical inheritance*. But it would take a huge step of obedience.

On a trip to Vietnam in 1994, I met a group of young people, on the streets of Saigon, wanting to practice their English. It turned into a meaningful conversation about Christ, and I was able to pray with them that they might know Jesus in a personal way. I then introduced them to some Vietnamese believers to continue their journey. That night in the hotel room, the Lord spoke clearly to my heart, saying, "Craig, you are pouring your life out in Manila, but you are missing Asia." This is not the place to tell that story, but by the following year, we had given away the Bible School, and I had become the Asia/Pacific Regional Director for Go To Nations. We had become very aware that the nations were in our hearts, and we were called to not just "go" but to keep going to those places least touched by the Gospel.

We began to pioneer and run Bible schools underground in Vietnam. As of this writing, we have over eleven hundred graduates all over that nation. And we continued to learn to cover ourselves, our family, the ministry, and our students in prayer with great success. As we only did what the Father asked us to do and prayed in obedience, we walked in divine protection, never had fear, and saw incredible results. By giving the first Bible School away, God gave us a model we had never seen before and went from just three couples and one quarterly underground Bible School in Vietnam to a team of about forty missionaries and almost thirty Bible Schools being run simultaneously throughout the region. *Then came Nepal.*

In 1999, I was high up in the foothills of the Himalayas in Northern Nepal. I was pretty sick from the water or altitude or a combination of the two. So, as the team moved up the mountain to witness to some monks in a Tibetan monastery, I sat on my poncho in the mist on the side of the road. As I looked out over peak after peak after peak of an almost entirely unreached people group, I simply said to the Lord, "How do I, as one man, have an impact on these nations?"

Immediately I heard in my spirit, "Ask of me, and I will give you the nations as your inheritance, the ends of the earth as your provision." I knew that Scripture. It is from Psalm 2:8. But I also knew that was written to, for, and about Jesus. Of course, He got the nations; He died on a cross to purchase them. That is what I said back to God. "That is—Jesus's verse. He died to purchase the nations."

Again, immediately, I heard this verse: "All things that the Father has are Mine. Therefore, I said that He will take of mine and declare it to you" (John 16:15, NKJV). The "He" in this verse is the Holy Spirit if you look at the chapter. What this verse is saying is that whatever belongs to the Father belongs to the Son, whatever belongs to the Son belongs to the Holy Spirit. And, did you get it? What belongs to the Holy Spirit belongs to you and me. What's His is mine because the Holy Spirit lives in me (and you).

As soon as I heard that verse, I heard this one, "And if children, then heirs; heirs of God, and joint-heirs with Christ; if so be that we suffer with him, that we may also be glorified together" (Rom. 8:17). All through the 1990s, I had been studying sonship. In this one divine moment, God wove what I had been learning (seeds of sonship) with an even greater truth—*biblical inheritance* available to those sons.

Inheritance in the Bible is twofold. First, to "inherit" means to drive out the previous tenant. Second, to "inherit" means to take possession of the territory or domain where the tenant has just been displaced. Displace and replace. In prayer, I can displace, but **in person**, I must replace. As I studied this for the next few months, I saw first of all that *biblical inheritance* is nations; that is what Jesus died for. It is people, people groups, and global families. God said to Abraham in Genesis 12, "all families on Earth will be blessed through you." That is the biblical end goal. That is *the* mandate from the river of Genesis 2 to the river of Revelation 22. That's why the church exists, to flow to the nations. *Look those rivers up.*

The second thing I soon learned is that *biblical inheritance* only goes to sons. We are all children of God, but many in the family never make it to sonship. Children ask God to bless what they are doing, but sons take responsibility for the family business, the "Father's business" as Jesus said. His business is nations. We don't get nations until we get in "the Father's business." My truth on sonship was being woven together with my truth on inheritance. To seal this revelation God was giving me, He had one more destiny-changing, life-defining "truth" in store.

I was reading through my Bible that year, from Genesis to Revelation, and it was December of 1999 when I came to this verse in Revelation 2:26–27. "And he that overcomes, and keeps my works unto the end, to him will I give power over the nations: And he shall rule them with a rod of iron; as the vessels of a potter shall they be broken to shivers: even as I received of my Father" (paraphrased). If you are familiar with Scripture, you may realize that verse 27 is a quote from Psalm 2:9. The verse that immediately follows the verse "Ask of me and I will give you the nations." **This is written in red, so it is Jesus speaking directly to us**, His sons and daughters.

If you add all of these verses together, what just happened in Revelation 2:27–28 is this: if we continue (as we have been talking about) and we keep "His works" (I believe that is John 4:34–35, the "work of the harvest"), then He authorizes us to claim what is rightfully His as co-destined heirs. In verse 28, He literally writes us (rights or authorizes us) **into the will.** This single truth—no longer a seed—revolutionized my life, our finances, and the entire global ministry.

With understanding, I began to ask for specific nations, and within a period of time, we would receive, through absolute divine appointment, a very legitimate invitation to come and establish ministry in the very nation we asked for. Not just a visit, a trip, or outreach. We have people living and growing ministry in almost every nation we have asked for at this point! Every nation belongs to Father as Creator/Owner in Genesis. Satan stole our inheritance from Adam in Genesis, but Jesus bought the nations back with His blood on the Cross. That means the nations are **twice** owned by God! Once as Creator and once as Redeemer.

As His sons and daughters, what belongs to Him belongs to us. We are authorized to inherit, displace, and replace. With this revelation and understanding, I began to fly into nations, and as the plane would land I would declare, "This is my Father's nation, He created it. My older brother Jesus purchased it with His own body and blood on the Cross. I am a son, an authorized representative of the family, about my Father's business, and I am here to take our nation back." That prayer when authorized by Heaven changes things! Glory to God! Nations came and are still coming. Influence came and continues to come. Laborers came and keep coming. Resources came and continue to come. All as a result of verbally declaring the scriptural revelation that had grown from seed to maturity in my own heart. *That is Authorized Governmental Anointing at the highest level.*

My seeds so became truth-bearing trees that I had to be wise in what I asked for. I did not ask for nations that we as a team were not ready in manpower and finance to step into. If you remember back to the Iraq war under President Bush, US troops rolled into Baghdad and toppled the statue of Saddam Hussein in twenty-one days! That is the same nation (Babylon) that Daniel prayed over for twenty-one days until there was a spiritual breakthrough. US troops "disinherited" an enemy government in twenty-one days, but years later we were, and in some ways still are, working to establish a "new culture" in that nation. That is a good picture, in our recent lifetime of how Kingdom works. We can pray and pray, but at some point, someone has to go and stay until Kingdom culture is established. That is a discipled nation as Jesus calls for in Matthew 28.

We only pray when we are ready to go and, more importantly, ready to stay. This same truth can apply to your family, your school, your city, your business, or whatever you hear God telling you to "take back from the enemy." Isaiah 1:19 says, "If you are **willing and obedient** you shall eat the good of the land." Understanding this was the next step, the next truth to getting more. Understanding the seed, understanding the "more to abundance" process. Understanding Kingdom rulership. Understanding application as sons gives us greater authorization. God was building a "case" file for the coming season. Isn't that what He is always doing, if we are seeking first the Kingdom, have ears to hear and eyes to see, and are **willing and obedient**?

The most recent nation I asked for was Myanmar. It was in 2014. Our Thailand team was conducting a leadership conference with many of our Thai and Burmese graduates in Thailand, right on the border of Myanmar. As we worshiped that morning, I knew in my heart it was time to ask for that nation. As I looked toward the foothills on the other side of the border I said, "God, give us Myanmar." Just that prayer. Simple, but from the context I am sharing here, I fully knew what it meant when I voiced that prayer. I know something is going to happen every time.

That was about nine o'clock in the morning. Just after noon, our Thailand director drove into the compound and was greeted by the Burmese pastor we have partnered with in Thailand for several years. The pastor walked right up to our director and said, "It's time. I want you to bring your team into Myanmar."

Three hours from my prayer of obedience to a personal invitation. *That is authorized governmental anointing, truth that is now working in abundance.* The very next year we had a Bible school inside Myanmar, and the year after that, another one. Our Thailand team conducted a crusade inside Myanmar last December. We are now established in that nation.

Biblical inheritance, as does any inheritance, comes with conditions, most of them based on character and Holy Spirit fruit that gives proof of sonship. The purpose of this book is not to expand on that theme, but to use the truth of that understanding, along with other truths, to make a case for the prayers in this book. "Son" in the New Testament is the Greek word *huios*, and it means "those that reflect the character and nature of their Father." Sons get to pray big prayers with big results. I have long said, "It pays to be a child of God. It costs to be a son." However, the rewards of being in the Father's business are global!

What we must recognize is that Holy Spirit gift and divine calling originate in Heaven as a testimony to the goodness of God and His desire to touch this earth. Gifts and calling have very little to do with "us" individually. What God is looking for in "sons" is character and fruit of the Holy Spirit. Let me give you a couple of examples.

Matthew 5:9, part of the Beatitudes, says this: "Blessed are the peacemakers, for they shall be called the sons of God." Sons display and promote peace. Galatians 3:29–4:7 is a pretty clear picture of what it means to be a child of God and what it means to be a son of God. In a few verses, we go from slaves to sons to heirs.

Another very important condition for inheritance is found in Romans 8:14 and confirms exactly what we are saying, "For as many as are **led by the Spirit of God**, these are the sons of God." That demonstration of Holy Spirit leadership is absolutely imperative to true spiritual authority and authorization as sons of God. Remember when Jesus was baptized in the Jordan River, the Father spoke from Heaven, saying, "This is my beloved son in whom I am well pleased." That was the authorization of Jesus as a matured son. At that point, and never before, Jesus was released into the Father's business. That is the established pattern God expects.

Then we read in Romans 8:17, "If we are children, then we are heirs, heirs of God, coheirs with Christ if we suffer with Him." We don't talk about the "suffering" part of this verse often, but it means "to carry the same burden, to experience the same kind of pain." Certainly, we are not going to the cross, so it is not talking about that. I believe what broke Jesus's heart was the lostness of man. Therefore, I believe in this verse, that "suffering" with Christ means getting under the burden of the lost.

You may have noted this verse is most often translated "children" instead of "sons." The Greek word in this verse is *teknon* and basically means "of legal age." Like a nearly adult teenager. This is the top end of the stage just prior to sonship. As an adult child, there is a legal right to pursue inheritance, as well as sonship. Neither inheritance nor sonship is given. They are both gained by pursuit. John 1:12 says, "But as many as received him, to them gave he the **power** to become the sons of God."

"Power" in this verse is the Greek word *exousia*. *Exousia* is the highest ordained power released by God for man to exercise on the earth. It has been described as "the legal right to do something (authority) as well as the might to see it done (power)." When Jesus gave the disciples the Great Commission in Matthew 28, this is the word for authority He used.

"All authority (*exousia*) in Heaven and Earth has been given to me." This is supreme spiritual authority. The authority of Jesus as the Son of God is the now-designated authority future sons are endued with as they step into place and take sonship responsibility.

It is "carrying the same burden" for souls, found in Romans 8:17; being about our "Father's Business," found in Luke 2:49; immersing ourselves in the "work of the Harvest," found in John 4:34–35; and contending with that "overcomers spirit" to the end, found in Revelation 2:26–27, that positions us to claim what is legally His.

This is what sets us up to pray authorized Kingdom or governmental prayers that shift things, change the atmosphere, correct the situation, open and close doors, and more. Sons and inheritance **always** go together. While I firmly believe the ultimate goal of all spiritual and *biblical inheritance* is souls and nations, in context, this same authority works in your home, your city, your business, or your environment.

A "family" in the Bible is simply a cultural group defined and bound together by certain traits. Today's teenagers would meet that definition. The men and women you work with would as well. God does not become exclusive in this case, but inclusive. An authorized son or daughter has every right to say, "This is my Father's city, this is my Father's school, this is my Father's company," and so on.

"Creation rights" make Him the owner of all things. As Creator in Genesis, our Father owns it all. Psalm 24:1 says the earth is the Lord's and all who dwell in it. Colossians 1 says everything was created by Him, every throne, every dominion, everything. To understand that means that anything built came from materials He placed here. All invention, creation, every compound, medicine, machinery, fiber, material, skyscraper, or sailboat started in the heart of God, and the ingredients were spoken into existence by His word.

How much more would this apply to people? Revelation 4:11 says we were created for His pleasure. For God so loved the world He gave His only Son to purchase us back from sin, from slavery of any kind, from social injustice, from political and spiritual regimes, and from poverty and sickness. "Your Kingdom come, Your will be done, on Earth as it is in Heaven, is what we are *authorized* to go after."

4

KNOWING YOUR SEASON
OR CHANGING IT

As I said in the introduction to this book, there are lots of ways to pray in the Bible, all of them correct, depending on what your assignment is, what the strategy of Heaven is for that assignment, and what season you are in. Let me give you an example.

In order to keep my slightly overcrowded garage as neat as is reasonably possible, I switch out some of what hangs on my walls depending on what season it is. For much of the year, my yard rake hangs in a very accessible place. But there comes a time late in the year when I put the yard rake in the attic and bring out the snow shovel to hang in its place. Both tools are incredibly valuable "in their season." "All kinds of prayer," as Paul says, is very much like that. Each has its assignment and its season. Too many believers are using the right tool in the wrong season. Knowing and yielding to the season we are in is absolutely critical to any kind of real Kingdom advancement. I heard Leif Hetland say, "If you don't know what season you are in, you don't know what your assignment is." Exactly.

The Bible makes mention of the sons of the tribe of Issachar in 1 Chronicles 12:32, stating that they "understood the times, with knowledge of what Israel should do." Today is not yesterday, and it is not tomorrow. Faith is now. Now is the time. His intent is that now, through the Church, the manifold wisdom of God should be made known (Eph. 3:10). We need a today-strategy that will align us with a tomorrow-opportunity.

Jesus said in John 8:58, "Before Abraham was, I am." Jesus was already standing in Abraham's future before Abraham was even born. I love that. God works out of our timeline. He is already standing in our tomorrows, waiting for us to align our hearts, minds, plans, and purposes with His. When our lives intersect the plans and purposes of God, in the timing of God, divine opportunities are going to be the result. The prayers we are talking about are calling this type of alignment into being.

There are tried-and-true weapons and they never fail. The Word of God, the blood of Jesus, and the Name of Jesus are all unstoppable. But knowing how and when to apply them increases their manifest power many times over. In the New Testament, you find all kinds of what I call prayer boosters, like "prayer and thanksgiving," "prayer and persistence," or "prayer and fasting."

Prayer and fasting in agreement with the timing of God is nation changing. I believe Isaiah 58 is the end goal of all fasting:

> Is this not the fast which I choose, to loosen the bonds of wickedness, to undo the bands of the yoke, and to let the oppressed go free and break every yoke? Is it not to divide your bread with the hungry and bring the homeless poor into the house; When you see the naked, to cover him; and not to hide yourself from your own flesh? Then your light will break out like the dawn, and your recovery will speedily spring forth; and your righteousness will go before you; the glory of the Lord will be your rear guard. Then you will call, and the Lord will answer; You will cry, and He will say, "Here I am." (NASB)

Prayer and fasting align both us and Earth with the plans, purposes, and pursuits of God. As our team was growing in the Philippines, we met weekly to pray in our living room, which became the "power base" for the entire ministry in the Asia/Pacific Region. We came to a season where I sensed the Lord drawing near. I have done a number of fasts over the years, and almost always I am drawn into them by a spiritual pull toward the Father. I have learned to lean into those and welcome them.

As I began to feel this pull, I simply said to our team, which was about twenty missionaries and apprentices at the time, "I believe the Lord is drawing near. Let's prepare our hearts and lean into that. Let's give ourselves to that." I don't remember if I even mentioned the word "fasting." I may have, but I didn't mandate anything, and we didn't make a "fasting schedule." But out of that drawing, team members began to fast. Unscripted. Unorganized by us. We were just following His drawing. Some did short fasts. Some did long fasts. But no one announced to anyone else what they were doing until they were already doing it.

Each week as we gathered to pray, someone would say, "I stopped my fast on this day." Then someone else would say, "I started a fast that same day." To the best of my memory, that fast continued for nearly a year. Unbroken. Incredible. Just purely the Holy Spirit setting us up for a coming season we were completely unaware of at the time. This is why our yielding to the timing of God in our current season is so critical to the coming one. God sets us up, but if we pass by these burning bush moments, we miss the breakthroughs God intends. Moments build momentum and become movements in the timing of God.

Thank God we caught our moment! In the midst of that season, during one of our regular weekly team prayer times, one of our young, apprenticing missionaries felt an unction from God. He said, "I believe God is saying that if we ask for a nation, He will give it to us." This was at least two years before my encounter in Nepal and the understanding of "claiming inheritance in the nations" I have now. I wasn't walking in that revelation yet. We did all we knew to do at the time. We simply waited on God, not wanting to ask out of presumption, our own intellect, or personal desires.

When God tells you to ask for something, the key to divine authorization is to ask for what He wants you to ask for. Find what is in His heart and go after it. Finally, after an uncomfortable time of silence and waiting, I said, "God, give us Thailand." When I said that, the Spirit of God fell in the room, and the team members began to cry out to God for Thailand for the better part of an hour. And that was that. Over the next couple of years, we made a few trips to Thailand, but nothing much happened, and we didn't try to make it happen in our own strength or ability.

Then after seven years, an invitation came. It was eight years from that "asking" to the day we put a missionary family on the ground in Thailand. That was our first ask, and short of the revelation we would later have. Nevertheless, Thailand today is our largest multi-cultural, multi-generational team anywhere in the world. From Thailand, we have broken into several surrounding nations and that continues. It is the epicenter for where we are spiritually and practically in Asia right now. **All** of that came from praying the right prayer at the right time in the right way. Timing.

As believers, we must take ownership of our season. I was flying from Bangkok to Saigon a few years ago. As we reached our cruising altitude, the Lord just dropped this on me: "Craig, you can change your season." I said, "What?" Again, He said, "You can change your season. Elijah did." Look it up. Elijah prayed it would stop raining and it did. Then having a Word from God and taking ownership of the Word and the timing, he engaged a "God Prayer Strategy," an authorized governmental prayer to call for rain again, and it rained. He changed the seasons twice at God's word.

Don't be victim to the season you are in, the financial situation you are in, the job situation you are in, and the nation you are in. If you don't like the atmosphere where you are—**change it.** That is what we are authorized to do as we grow in understanding, faith, obedience, and responsibility. Authorized, authorized, authorized. That is what the New Testament is all about. And now is the time for us to exercise our God-given, Christ-proven, cross-purchased authority.

You are here now, and we all have an expiration date, so **now** is your time. I have simply prayed "Your Kingdom come" again and again and watched people's lives shift, watched obstacles move out of the way, and watched doors open that were tightly closed. Knowing your authorization, knowing your assignment, knowing your season, and knowing your strategic weapon all converge to release the atmosphere of Heaven into our family, city, business, nation, government, and world.

I like to use both Moses and David as examples when we talk about the timing of God. Moses received instructions and oversaw the building and establishment of the tabernacle of Moses. But where do you find Moses? And where do you find David? You find them both in personal prayer tents, having face-to-face meetings with God. Under Old Testament law, that was impossible. Unholy men could not meet face-to-face with a Holy God. Yet they did. What Moses and David did was pull the New Testament God of grace into their seasons, thousands—**thousands**—of years before it was theologically possible. That is the power of knowing God and knowing your season. Tomorrow is entirely possible today if we are properly aligned with His heart, mind, plans, and purposes!

Ecclesiastes 8:6 is another verse that makes clear the critical need for the timing of God. "For there is a proper time and procedure for every delight (matter), though a man's trouble (misery) is heavy upon him." In God's timing, the right things happen. In our own timing, it is pretty miserable. God's timing is full measure in every matter.

"Your Kingdom Come, Your will be done, on Earth as it is in Heaven." **Now**. Lean into this emerging season. Something Heaven sent is unfolding all around us, and if we engage where God is going, it will be a destiny-changing ride of global proportions.

5

GOVERNMENTAL ANOINTING

We have been working toward laying a solid foundation with enough revelation to cause you to feel authorized to go after some greater things in prayer. Let's look specifically at what it means to pray governmental prayers.

You should start in Genesis because the entire power/authority structure for the earth is established in those first three chapters. Myles Monroe does an excellent job with this in his book, *Understanding the Purpose and Power of Prayer*. In Genesis chapter 1, when God created Adam and Eve, the first recorded spoken words out of God's mouth were "Let them have dominion." As His creation, we have a domain, and we are created to dominate in our domain. Theologically, God rules over the earth, but man was created and established in a stewardship role to rule on the earth.

Genesis 2:15 says God "set" man in the garden. Adam was not created there. He wasn't just a fruit or product of what God was creating. He was created outside of the garden and "set in" as a picture of authorized dominion. That picture is the first picture of what God intends his sons' and daughters' roles to be in the earth. Wherever you are "set" by God is your domain; you are authorized to spiritually rule the environment. Tend to it. Take care of it—whether you are working in a day care or running your own corporation.

Adam lost that authority as the first man, and then "the man Christ Jesus," fully God and fully man, came and took it back. Because a "man" gave it away, a "man" had to take it back. Once He did, through His death, burial, and resurrection, everything changed. Jesus is now fully authorized and so has every right to authorize you and me to work on His behalf in this earth.

Isaiah 9 is a great picture of what we have been saying: "Unto us a child is born, unto us a son is given: and the government shall be upon His shoulder." You see that? A child was born, but He was not given to us until He was *huios*, a mature son, reflecting the character and nature of his Father. It is at sonship level that the government of God is established. The government of God rests on His shoulders, as this verse clearly states.

What that does is set the stage for "positional authority." Jesus is now exalted, as the King of all kings, Lord of all lords, seated at the right hand of God in supreme authority (Col. 3:1). To "sit down" means "it is set-tled, done, finished." Jesus rules from a seated position. What does that mean to us? Well, it means that we actually live in two places at the same time. We are most certainly here on Earth, but Ephesians 2:6 says, "God has raised us up *with Christ* and seated us with him in the heavenly realms in Christ Jesus." Since I am "in Christ," then spiritually I have every right to operate, in prayer especially, from the throne of Christ.

Acts 17:28 says, "For in him we live, and move, and have our being." If I am living and moving "in him," where is He? In Heaven. Colossians 3:3 says, "My life is now hidden with Christ in God." Wow! We have to change where we think from, look from, and operate from. Instead of working from the earth to the throne, especially where and when prayer is concerned, we have been fully authorized to work from the throne of Christ to the earth.

Part of governmental prayer is "shouldering the season," "shouldering the mantle," or "shouldering the assignment." We become yoked together with Him in the season's assignment to see His Kingdom come, His will be done on Earth as it is in Heaven. God, through Christ, begins to speak through us, declaring and decreeing His Word and His will into the domains we steward in the earth.

To me, as I began to use the words "Governmental Anointing," it meant "an assignment, *and the mantle or equipment* and authorization to fulfill that assignment in prayer, at a government level." I believe a mantle is an equipping for an impending assignment. I also believe that mantles are not made to fit us, but that we are made to fit mantles. David tried on Saul's armor, but it was too big. Or David was too small for a king's authority at that time! I believe we grow into mantles as we mature spiritually. When we "fit it," we "get it." BAM! And something changes in our authority level. The same prayers get different results because we are "mantled" for the assignment.

We were seeing all these truths working, and our understanding was growing in all of these areas we are talking about in this book. But I was being pulled into a much higher arena—one in which prayers could be made that affected decisions at a much higher spiritual and earthly governmental level. With all of these things in mind, I was regularly asking God for a governmental anointing, a mantle and authorization from Heaven to see change in places where physically or socially I had no previous influence.

In 2013, I was again in a season of fasting. This time I was traveling in Asia, and I do not like traveling from nation to nation while fasting. But I knew God was in it. We were conducting an internship for beginning missionaries in the central Philippines, and I was part of the leadership team teaching the classes. It was a shifting season, and both the Vice President of the ministry at the time, Nancy Lovelace (now Executive Vice President), and I recognized that God was at work. While Nancy was teaching one morning, I was in my room praying in the midst of this fasting season. I was walking back and forth past the end of my bed, and each time I crossed the center line, I could feel an incredible weight on my shoulders. So eventually I took a chair and sat down right where I felt the weight. Weight almost always represents the glory of God. Glory can be translated as "weight" in some cases. Weight on the shoulders often represents the government of God because the government is on His shoulders as Isaiah 9 says.

As I fervently prayed that morning, I said out of my mouth, "God, I want a governmental anointing." Immediately I felt led to read Isaiah 45. Isaiah 45 is about King Cyrus, who was not a believer, but as you read the account, he was greatly used by God. God's "hand" was on Cyrus, meaning God authorized him for the season. I did some study in *Holman's Bible Dictionary* and found that Cyrus truly was a warrior/king. As king, he routed the then powerful Babylonian empire and greatly expanded the territory under his dominion. He became known for his powerful military exploits and for establishing significant policies of peace in the region.

As I began to read Isaiah 45, this is what I found:

> This is what the Lord says to His anointed, to Cyrus, whose right hand (the hand of authority) I take hold of to subdue nations before him and to strip kings of their armor, to open doors before him so that gates will not be shut: I will go before you and will level the mountains, I will break down gates of

bronze and cut through bars of iron. I will give you hidden treasures (souls?), riches stored in secret places, so that you may know that I am the Lord, the God of Israel, who summons you by name. (NIV)

Immediately I knew that I was being "authorized" at an entirely greater level. That was the anointing I had been contending for, for two decades.

As the Regional Director for Go To Nations, I had also appointed and authorized leaders all over Asia. If God was authorizing me at a greater level, then it would begin to flow to them as well. Not long after that, I began to hear stories of our team leaders, especially in Thailand, experiencing some unusual results in their ministry efforts. I heard a number of stories of team members who had gone to government offices requesting favor, requesting the right to do something, requesting authorization for an event, an outreach, and so on. Several times as they approached an official, they were immediately told, "We can't do that. You can't be here. We are closed now," or something similar to that. But in each case, as the official was speaking and saying no with his mouth, they were signing official paperwork that said yes. It happened again and again and again. What an amazing Father!

As I was growing in this, it began to happen to us as well. We had a long season of working with insurance companies as so many things were changing in this last season and it was very frustrating. We couldn't get answers. Sandra spent hours and days on the phone, and it was going nowhere. Finally, my spirit had had enough, and I said "no more." I began to call upon a governmental anointing and command things to come into line. Things began to shift. We were able to get insurance. Doors opened up. It took some time, but things began to move forward. We were not victims of a huge government-orchestrated health care system. It wasn't overnight, but it moved and changed to meet our needs.

Then Sandra took a trip to Thailand and ended up with blood clots in her legs. We had health insurance and trip insurance, and both said they would not pay. Being out of the country became the disqualifying factor for Sandra's health insurance, and the possibility of any "pre-existing conditions" let the trip insurance off the hook also. It wasn't a staggering bill, but with several weeks under medical care in Bangkok, the bill was roughly $13,000. Enough to pray about. So I went to war, praying governmentally, "Your Kingdom come, Your will be done." Again, it took weeks and weeks, several phone calls, and written appeals. God does His part, but we have to do ours too. "Those that are led by the Spirit are sons." The Spirit knows what to pray, how to pray, and when to pray. He also knows what He must do and what we must do. It takes both, and we have to be "willing and obedient."

Finally, after a couple of months, we received a letter in the mail from the trip insurance company explaining in detail that they were not paying and why they were not paying. The very next piece of mail that I opened came the exact same day from the exact same company, and in that envelope was a check for the entire amount! While they said they would not, they did. Governmental anointing.

This continued to happen in both big and small ways for about a year. It was a learning curve, but it was fun to hear no and see yes. We were getting breakthroughs, big ones.

Then, early in 2015, there was a significant shift in the entire ministry. We had continued to seek God for prayers and strategies that would "break down gates of bronze and cut through bars of iron" as Isaiah 45:2 says. Once again we were in Thailand, meeting with our team, praying, and establishing Kingdom stuff in that nation. As I was leaving a powerful meeting with our team, the Lord spoke very clearly to me these words: "It is time to declare, decree, proclaim, and prophesy."

This time I had a pretty clear understanding of what that meant. But to be sure I got it, a couple of weeks later I opened an article written by Dutch Sheets about *kingly prayers and intercession*. In that article, he stated almost word for word something the Lord had spoken to me. He said the Lord had said to him, "It is time to declare, decree, proclaim, and prophesy." Okay, God had my attention. So I began to study.

When God gives us specific words, those words have meaning and carry significance in the spiritual realm. It is imperative that we know and understand exactly what God is asking or directing us to do.

Then we are able to align our practices with His purposes in faith and confidence. Dutch gives us a brief explanation of what these powerful words mean: "Decrees (official orders, edicts or decisions), declarations (announcements or formal statements), and proclamations (the process of binding and loosing) as we are prophetically inspired by Holy Spirit to do so." Dutch continues, "The power of God's decreed word is extraordinary! It releases His creativity, His salvation, and yes, His judgments! He rules through His words, and so must we." Amen.

In Revelation 1:6, it says, "He has made us to be both kings and priests." A priestly role or responsibility is to petition Heaven on behalf of Earth. That is an intercessor's role. And as I have said, this is one more example of the right kind of prayer in the right season. However, a king declares over the earth on behalf of Heaven, proclaiming the will of Heaven over the situation. This is sometimes called apostolic prayer, because the original apostle's role is very governmental in nature, and Jesus is the Apostle and High Priest of our confession (Heb. 3:1). It is also sometimes called prophetic prayer, as we declare the will of Heaven over Earth, partnering with God to align and decree into the future. To "prophesy" can mean to foretell or tell forth the future. Prophetic declarations call the future into biblical Kingdom alignment.

The Lord had said to Dutch specifically that it was time to lay down priestly intercession and time to take up kingly intercession. Since seeds had been planted in me for more than two decades now, I immediately understood that part of the "expectation" God had spoken to us back in the 1990s was now being called into place through a season of "declaration." God was expecting more in prayer, and I should expect more in results.

In a short period of time, all I had been learning came together into a focused prayer strategy for this season, as we say on the cover of the book *Essential Prayer Strategies for an Unprecedented Hour.*

One very significant answer to prayer came again with our Thailand team. We have a wonderful American couple on the team, who had already adopted a son from Thailand years before they joined us and moved to Thailand as missionaries. Shortly after their arrival in Thailand, a very challenged Thai family asked our missionaries to care for their young granddaughter. The grandmother, who had become disabled due to a stroke, had more than she could handle in caring for her granddaughter and was desperate for help. She saw this couple, with a Thai son already, who might be an answer.

The couple counseled with us, and we felt God was in it. (I want to note that the couple and the Thai family followed steps to submit the situation to the Department of Social Welfare. The Lord showed me years prior that you cannot challenge the authority of the devil in these nations unless you are submitting to the laws of that land, when they do not oppose God's Word. Scripture is clear that authority is established by

God, and we can't cut corners and walk in divine authority. By submitting to the process and following the law, the child was placed in their care through the adoption center.)

They fostered this young child for quite some time while beginning to navigate the uncertain adoption process. It is a **huge** thing to adopt while living in these nations. We prayed, and we all felt it was God. So they started a long and arduous process. I won't give the details here, but it was years that we kept it in prayer.

Along the way, the process began to really bog down, and they were being stonewalled and ignored in the Social Welfare System. In prayer, I saw that what they were doing in the natural, adopting an unwanted child in Thailand, was a prophetic act that would go to the root of the orphan spirit in that nation and release the spirit of adoption in a greater measure. They weren't adopting for that reason; they simply loved this daughter and welcomed her into their family. But God was using their sacrifice, devotion, love, and integrity to do far more.

Almost two years into the process, everything had stopped. Their social worker would not return calls. The paperwork was just sitting, and the family had reason to believe that their file may have been lost. I felt that same spiritual weight on my shoulders that it was time to "govern" this. I began to pray. In prayer, I saw a bony, withered hand resting on top of a stack of papers. Clearly, the enemy was using someone to hold this adoption back. I took authority over whatever power that was and began to declare and decree God's Word and will over the matter.

Within weeks, the couple was able to contact their social worker; their file was found, completely in order, and things began moving again until the adoption was completed in a timely manner. We do our part; He does His part, with authority, at a governmental level when God's plans and purposes are hindered.

6

DECLARE AND DECREE

Job 22:28 says, "You will also decree a thing, and it will become established for you" (NASB). "Thing" in this verse can mean "a promise, a command, a decree, an argument, a speech." A "thing" is anything from a promise to a speech. As I said in the introduction, we don't get to just make things up and throw them out there and expect God to move. But when we are listening to the Holy Spirit, our hearts are aligned with God's plans and purposes. And when we are seeking first the Kingdom of God, He indeed expects us to speak out in faith, declaring and decreeing both His Word and His will.

In the middle of this process and before the Lord had spoken to me directly about "declaring and decreeing," I was walking in the growing revelation I had at the time. One of the things that dropped into my spirit for my own adult son, daughters, and their spouses was "pro." I began to declare "pro" over each one of them. They were all in frustrating jobs, looking for other opportunities and in need of increased income. For me, "pro" meant promotions, raises, and opportunities. It was something I declared regularly for several months.

One by one, things began to change with our children and their spouses. Our son received two or three significant raises over a several month period. He didn't ask. The raises just came and changed his income in a measurable way. His wife, our daughter-in-law, received a couple of new job opportunities in that same season and was offered a job that let her leave her current position and start brand new with another well-established business at the same level of pay and highly increased benefits. She was now positioned for increase, whereas in her previous job she was near the ceiling of her potential. In less than a year, she was asked to be on the interview committee for new applications. Divine favor.

Our son-in-law and youngest daughter also had some meaningful job offers. One worked out but did not last, and one was lost at the last moment. I saw in both of those that God had set our children up and provided divine opportunities, but the will of man had gotten in the way and disrupted what I believe was the plan of God for both of them. As powerful as these prayers are, they are spiritual in nature, and you can't always control what men will decide to do. I could have left these out and painted a picture that every declaration we make is going to be just what we call into place. But no one gets every prayer answered to our liking, and God always knows things we don't that may affect short-term outcomes in view of long-term goals.

But overall, we have seen so many answered prayers and much quicker results using these prayers that we know are ordained in this season. In this particular case, I can't give you Scripture and verse for God being "pro." But you have to know His heart and intent. We have a good understanding of the will of God throughout Scripture. It does say He desires to bless us and that His blessings will come upon us and overtake us as we walk in obedience. He wants us to prosper as our souls are prospering. You begin to speak those things that demonstrate the nature of God while staying true to Scripture. Sons reflect the character and nature of their Father.

In Job 22:28, to "decree" means to cut down and destroy or to decide. A decree can have a positive impact on a negative thing by seeing it cut down or destroyed. Or you can agree with God's Word, and by declaring it with authority and understanding, you are deciding with God for good in a situation. It is like a judge declaring a verdict. Psalm 119:89 says, "Forever, O Lord, Your word is settled in Heaven." "Settled" in this verse is past tense. It is over, done, finished. It is up to us to declare to be true in reality, what God already promised by His Word.

Isaiah 22:22 says, "I will place on His shoulder the key of the house of David, what He opens no one can shut, and what He shuts no one can open" (NIV). Remember that the government is on His shoulder, according to Isaiah 9:6. If you continue into verse 7, it says this: "Of the increase of his government and peace there shall be no end, upon the throne of David, and upon his kingdom, to order it, and to establish it with judgment and with justice from henceforth even forever."

We may not have seen it this way before, but in the context of what we are learning, you can see the biblical possibilities of what it means to "order" and "establish" through our scriptural decrees and declarations. Somewhere in this learning season, I was in Bhutan. Bhutan is a locked-down Tibetan Buddhist kingdom hidden away in the Himalayas. When we were there, we found there were less than two thousand known believers in the entire nation. Christians we met told us they had to stop burying their dead because the Tibetan monks dug them up and carved their thigh bones into flutes to conjure demons. As soon as our plane hit Bhutan's airspace, you could feel the demonic oppression.

One effect of Buddhism combined with the demonic was a valley full of stray mongrel dogs. We were told there were more dogs than people in the capital city. As soon as the sun went down, they would begin to howl and bark, and it would last all night. Demon dog barking is not fun when you are trying to sleep. I had been teaching from Creation in line with some of the things I have shared here—that we are authorized to rule on the earth, and that includes nature when necessary. Jesus calmed storms and called in fish. So that is biblical.

As I lay in bed hearing these dogs moan and growl and howl, I simply had enough and spoke out from the guest room I was staying in, "Dogs, I command you in the name of Jesus to be silent." Nothing happened. But I felt that God was in this, and I wasn't just making this up. I said again, "I am authorized by Heaven, I command you in the name of Jesus to be silent." Nothing happened. So a third time, I declared, "In the name of Jesus I command you dogs to be silent." I tell you as truth the whole valley went entirely silent. Not a whine, not a whimper. It was powerfully silent. A wonderful experience. As I began to doze off I heard in the distance the slightest howl, and I said, "In Jesus's name." It went silent and remained that way the rest of the night as far as I know. I woke up to peace and quiet the next morning.

I would like to say that that happens every time I pray, but it doesn't. However, I do believe that we get these glimpses into glory, these moments that allow us to see what "Your Kingdom come, Your will be done, on Earth as it is in Heaven" is supposed to look like. These moments are meant to build faith for movements.

In Matthew 16:18–19, as Jesus is establishing the New Testament Church, He is very clear. He says, "I give *you* the keys of the Kingdom…whatever *you* bind on Earth will be bound in Heaven, and whatever *you* loose on

Earth will be loosed in Heaven." Through this verse, we understand that we, the church, His sons, and daughters, are authorized to partner with Heaven to decide on matters concerning the will of God, their limitation or release in the earth, and call them into effect. When we agree with Heaven, the matter has already been agreed to as far as Heaven is concerned.

The word "declare" in the New Testament often simply means "announce." "Decrees" are faith-filled statements that apply the intent, will, and even text of God's Word to a situation. Declaration is announcing what God says to be true about a matter, again based on his intent, will, and Word. We decide, aligned with God, as co-destined heirs, what His will is in a situation and call it forth, declaring it to be so.

As we consider a king's role based on Revelation 1:6, just how would a king approach almost any situation? Kings don't often make appeals or requests, especially in matters of law. They do indeed make declarations and decrees. Kings speak in accordance with the established laws of the governments they represent. In Matthew 16, as Jesus is establishing the New Testament Church, He once again takes what is His from Isaiah 22:22 and authorizes the church, us, His sons and daughters, to use the keys of designated authority to move the will of Heaven forward and advance his Kingdom in the earth.

This then, in its entirety, line upon line, precept upon precept, establishes our kingly anointing in this hour to declare and decree the purposes of God over those things God desires to align for His glory in this hour. I love what Habakkuk 2:14 says, "For the earth shall be filled with the glory of the Lord as the waters cover the sea." I believe that is God's heart, His eternal intent as far as Earth is concerned—that the knowledge of God would be spread abroad in home after home, city after city, and nation after nation so that eternal choices can be made.

As this season was shifting and I recognized it, the Lord used this very verse with me. He spoke to my heart one day and said, "Craig, it's a new season, but for the same reason that the earth might be filled with the knowledge of the glory of the Lord, as the waters cover the sea."

Look at 2 Corinthians 5:17–20 (NIV):

> Therefore, if anyone is in Christ, the *new creation* has come: The old has gone, the new is here. All this is from God, who reconciled us to Himself through Christ and gave us the *ministry of reconciliation*: that God was reconciling the world to Himself in Christ, not counting people's sins against them. And He has committed to us the *message of reconciliation*. We are therefore *Christ's ambassadors*, as though God were making His appeal through us.

Every "new creation" has a "ministry" and stewards the "message" of the Kingdom. An ambassador's role is an authorized role, committed to declare and decree the will of the government he or she represents. It is time for the body of Christ to take responsibility as sons in the Father's business. We must agree with God's Word and allow ourselves to be rightly positioned as members of God's household, the royal family. As royal ambassadors, we must act on our Father's behalf to see His interest and desires released for our families and for His in every corner of the globe.

7

MAPS, BLUEPRINTS, AND KEYS

In this chapter, I want to give some strategic guidelines for applying what we are learning in this book. Authorized prayers, even a book on authorized prayers, is not an end in and of itself. The goal of any prayer should be a tangible demonstration of the Kingdom of God on Earth.

As we move to the end of this book and start praying governmental prayers, what is it we are truly expecting? How do those prayers become tools in seeing something born of God released in our home, school, city, state, or nation? That is where we need to be going in this hour.

I want to use this process first brought to my attention by our Southeast Asia West Regional Director, Ariel Acuna. Ariel was a relatively new believer when he found our first Go To Nations Bible School in Manila in the early

1990s. After graduation, Ariel has had an incredible story of pioneering ministry, which resulted in a church plant inside one of the Philippines' largest penal colonies. Then he planted and established several churches around his province. At the same time, he operated a number of our Bible schools to raise up workers not only for his own churches but for other churches and ministries as well.

Ariel understands apostolic pioneering. He moved with his wife and children to Thailand more than a decade ago to become our team leaders. He began to test the waters and read the spiritual climate. We could write an entire book on what Ariel has launched and continues to forge in Asia, Latin America, and North America. He understands establishing ministry in a challenging environment and has developed proven steps to set the stage for impact. What he is doing has worked in the Philippines, Thailand, and Myanmar so far. And Ariel's short list for the future includes some pretty difficult nations.

In 2014, as we were coming to more fully understand how God was authorizing us, Ariel did a brief devotional for our Thailand team about Maps, Blueprints, and Keys. It immediately caught my spirit, and I asked Ariel to more fully develop what God was giving him so it could be taught to the entire team in our 2015 Thailand team meeting. Ariel did just that, and in fact, it may have been the session he taught with this understanding that preceded God speaking to me about a declarative season.

I want to use Ariel's understanding to help set a framework for anyone reading this book to move their prayers toward expected and targeted results. What is God saying to you or to your church? What is God breathing on? Is there anything that keeps you awake at night or burns in you? First of all, you have to find that point where your life purpose (or ministry purpose) intersects the purposes of God in the earth for this generation (Acts 13:36).

Remember that purpose and destiny are two different things. David was in his purpose as a shepherd boy, a lion killer, a giant killer, a musician, and a warrior. But his destiny was to be king. We all have seasons of purpose throughout our lives building toward the destiny God has for us. Knowing your purpose in this season begins to give you a spiritual map. A map is a general direction for where you are going. Does God want to see a movement in your high school? Do you want to see the government in your city, county, or state changed? Is there something happening in your area that needs to stop, like the drug den in our subdivision? Is there something in your area that needs to be released, like a new economic engine to advance what God desires to do? What is God calling you to?

To move toward that, you need a map, a general sense of direction. Sort of a big picture connection to something God would like to do in the earth in partnership with you. A spiritual map is your starting point, but having a sense of direction, no matter how clear or detailed, is not enough. Now, there must be a blueprint or a divine strategy.

Knowing a flood is coming is one thing. Knowing we need to build a boat is an entirely different matter. Knowing we have a president that is with us, or against us as seasons change, is just a map. What is the divine strategy or the blueprint that lets us see the Kingdom advance in that season? Do we need to start something? Talk to someone? Build a team? Target something very specific and strategic in prayer? This is where we need Holy Ghost ideas. Remember that whatever is born of God overcomes in this world (1 John 5:4). Keep pressing in prayer until you see divine strategy. There is not one thing we face on this earth that God does not have a solution for. And the devil does not have a weapon that stops the Holy Spirit. We just need eyes to see and ears to hear what He is saying in this hour. Get with God until you get a spiritual strategy.

The final key then is just that, a **key**. Keys always represent designated authority. If I give you the keys to my car, it means I expect you to use it. You are authorized. We have a good friend that loans us his condo on the Gulf Coast each year. In his name, we are authorized and given the keys. We have full use of the place and all that goes with it. We are authorized in a general way throughout the New Testament. But specific strategies take specific keys. Locks are not one size key fits all.

Look at battle plans and how the Hebrew children took nations in the Old Testament. Sometimes they sent the worshippers out first. That was the key to that battle. Sometimes they fasted and prayed for three days before they went, another key. Sometimes the priest went with the Ark of the Covenant, a different key. Sometimes the leader stood on top of the mountain with his hands raised to the sky, yet another key.

Every map is different. Every strategy is different. Every key is different. Different locks mean different keys. Paul says in 1 Corinthians 16:9, "There are great doors of opportunity opened to me, but there are those that oppose me" (paraphrased). All around us are doors of opportunity for Christ to change lives, but those are not automatic. All opportunities come with opposition. The greater the opportunity usually means the greater the opposition.

You are going to have to contend for not just the strategy, but for the designated authority to do something about it. As you follow the flow of this book, the truth I had at each level would take me so far, but not until I prayed, "God, I want a governmental anointing" did I get the designated authority to go after things at a greater level. Every Christian has more authority than they will ever know. But as we are given divine assignments and accept the responsibility for those as part of the family business, it takes a greater level of authorization.

I just said to our team in Thailand, "It is like this. We all work at the Pentagon. We are all authorized to enter the building and work on behalf of our government in the arena of global peace and security. But there are rooms you can go into that others cannot. And there are rooms I can go into that some of you cannot." We get security clearance or authorization at greater levels based on our commitment to the cause, our ownership of the vision, our proven faithfulness and stewardship of previous assignments, and our strategic understanding of what each level's mission is. We all have keys, but to get into "that room" takes "the key."

If you believe God gave you the map, and you believe you have the blueprint or strategy to go after it, then you are going to have to contend until you get the specific key or keys it takes to unlock what needs to be unlocked. Remember Matthew 16, the formation of the New Testament Church. The Church is the gatekeeper of your city. The church is authorized to shut some gates and lock ungodly stuff out of the city. The church is also authorized to unlock and release some of what God has for that city.

If you do a deep dive on what "church" really means in the New Testament, using some good tools like a lexicon (*Thayer's Greek–English Lexicon of the New Testament*), you find a much richer meaning of what we commonly understand as "church." Church was not a spiritual word in Jesus's day. It was a sociopolitical term. The Greek word for "church" is *ekklesia*. In

54

Rome, the world power of the day, an *ekklesia* was "a called out assembly convened to deliberate the public affairs of a free state." The *ekklesia* had a very social and governmental role. Kevin Conner does an outstanding job of laying this out in his manual on *The New Testament Church*.

To summarize, the Roman *ekklesia* elected officials, directed city affairs, declared war on enemies, appointed military officers, assigned troops, and raised and allocated funds. What Jesus was saying, in essence, is that I will establish and build my *ekklesia*, my governing assembly in the city, and they will decide on matters concerning the well-being, safety, and atmosphere of the city. My church will open the right gates and close the wrong ones, and hell won't be able to stop them. This is why you have those keys. **Use them.**

A church with the right spiritual map, divine strategy, and designated keys for their city could do what the disciples did in Acts 17:6. That handful of men turned the world as they knew it upside down in less than a generation. A prayer group with the right map, strategy, and keys could see their high school changed. A husband and wife with the right map, strategy, and keys could see their entire family changed.

Years ago, after our son finished a year of college, he struggled for a season just to find his purpose and get established. I was praying against generational curses and anything working against him to hinder him from flourishing. One day as I was praying, the Lord spoke to me and said, "Craig, read the verse." I did a double take. "What Lord?" He said again, "Read the rest of the verse."

I looked up Exodus 20:5. It says that the sins of the fathers are visited on the children until the third and fourth generations. But verse 6 says, "God shows love to a thousand generations of those that love him and keep his commandments." I was breaking curses, but when I read this, God said, "Bless your children with what you have."

I thought about that for a while and then started making a list of all that God had blessed me with. Any revelation I walked in. Any blessing I had been given. Any sin or weakness I had seen broken. Any victory or triumph I walked in. Everything I could list that God, Christ, and the Holy Spirit had done in me over three decades. I crafted a prayer of blessing based on any spiritual truth I walked in and began to speak it over all three of our children. I can truly say we saw the most significant change and growth in our children in the next short season than we have seen in their entire lives.

Why? One, because God's Word accomplishes what He sent it to do. Two, because we were longing, desiring to see God work, and God always honors true spiritual hunger. Third, because we had a map of direction, a destination we wanted to get to. Fourth, we had a blueprint, a way of seeing that accomplished. And fifth, we had the keys. God spoke to my heart that the key was not going after the wrong, but releasing the blessing of what I carried over them.

The blessing is always more powerful than the curse. Life always overcomes death as far as God is concerned. Light is always more powerful than darkness. Divine strategies return divine results.

I pray that God will lay upon your heart some seeming impossibilities He wants to partner with you and others to see changed. May God give you the maps, blueprints, and keys to see His Kingdom come. His will be done, in those things that concern you, and those things that concern Him. In Jesus's name.

8

GOVERNMENTAL FAVOR

Before we move to the prayers in this book, I want to share something I have recognized as a result of operating in a governmental anointing, and that is governmental favor. As I began to order our affairs and declare and decree according to Scripture, there was an unexpected and rather astonishing side effect I call governmental favor.

In Scripture, "favor" and "grace" are often interchangeable words. Grace can simply mean that God does for us what we cannot do for ourselves. It is an extension of His goodness and expresses unlimited love that empowers us to do what He asks us to. As things began to shift and move, and opportunities opened up, favor began to just show up, as others did for us what we could not do for ourselves.

For example, as all of our insurance was getting on track and working, we began to get calls from various health care and pharmaceutical companies. They would call and ask for Sandra, and then they would tell her they had been working on her account and had found a grant that would cover her current prescription cost. We didn't apply for anything. We hadn't asked for anything. Someone, somewhere, for some reason, went to work for us, without us asking, and found solutions we didn't even know existed. Governmental anointing releases governmental favor.

We have seen it time and time again in all kinds of ways over the past two years. When God moved through governmental decrees and declarations on behalf of our missionaries for adopting a child in Thailand things began to happen. Their social worker called them, began to move paperwork, set up appointments, and arranged the final meetings. She did for them what they could not do for themselves.

Most recently, Sandra and our daughter-in-law were looking at a private Christian school for our grandson, their son, who is about to start first grade. Sandra has been homeschooling him as she did with all of our children in preparation for school. This particular school came highly recommended, and they had visited the school and met the administrator, teachers, and other staff. It was decided our grandson would start there in first grade.

It would be expensive the first year, but our home state has a voucher system. After the first year, our grandson would be eligible for the state voucher that would cover most of his annual tuition, and with an available scholarship, by second grade the cost of this private Christian school would be reasonable. Sandra began to set some money aside to help pay for the first year. The paperwork was done, and our grandson was on the list for first grade.

Then, completely unexpectedly, Sandra received a phone call from the school administrator. This is what she said to Sandra: "I have been looking, and I think I found a loophole." Sandra didn't even know what she was talking about. We hadn't asked for any favors. We didn't say, "Oh, that is expensive. Can we get a discount?" We trusted God. We knew He would provide. So we hadn't said a word.

But for some (divine) reason, this young lady had been looking for ways to get our grandson into the school at a discount. She had taken it upon herself and been working and working. She found that if he enrolled by the end of March and graduated after completing the last eight weeks of kindergarten, he would qualify for all state vouchers and would go to first grade free. We had about two weeks to get him started.

The cost for the last two months of school would be $700, but the school offers enrolled students an annual scholarship of $500, so he would pay $200 for two months of private school and then start first grade at

little or no cost. Not only that, when his younger brother starts school, he will already qualify and won't have to pay from the very beginning. Governmental favor!

We didn't ask for that and weren't specifically looking for it, but someone else did for us what we could not do for ourselves. That is favor, governmental favor, where God works through others on our behalf. I believe that as we continue to apply these prayer principles and put these decrees and declarations into action, unmerited favor will begin to flow in ways never seen before. That is what we are experiencing personally, and God is no respecter of persons. He always rewards faith and obedience.

A good friend of ours, partner and prayer warrior, signs all of her e-mails this way. *Live expectantly*! As we get ready to embark on a new prayer season and an unfolding of Heaven's plan for this hour, I want to take that a step further and speak over you—*pray expectantly*!

Heaven is on the move in the earth as never before. **Now is the time!**

9

USING THIS BOOK

In the final section of this book, there are five specific prayers. The first is a prayer of repentance and agreement to set our hearts right before we move on. Following that are four specific prayers of declarations and decrees focusing on four different aspects we are going after.

The first declaration prayer was written late in 2015 and was active all through 2016 and forward. Here is where we have the most experience, and the results were significant enough; we knew it was God's strategy. Several of the testimonies in this book are a result of this prayer.

The second declaration prayer is for our government and our leaders. I felt very strongly that I needed a strategic prayer strategy after the election in 2016. The Lord spoke very directly to me that the election was not the end, but just the beginning, and even more prayer was needed after the election than before.

The third declaration prayer was built around some of the things this ministry, Go To Nations, does that are specifically aimed at impacting the nations of the earth. Historically, Go To Nations has worked in over ninety-six nations, five out of the seven continents, and currently serves in over forty-four nations. As Vice President of the Ministries Division, I have spiritual oversight for all of that. At the same time, **every son and daughter** are legally authorized by Christ to claim nations, to go personally or to send others in their place.

The fourth declaration prayer was written early in 2017 in response to some perhaps world-changing business ventures that some of our board members and business friends were moving toward and the promise of Deuteronomy 8:18. I lay out the biblical precedent for Kingdom finance and marketplace ministry in the introduction to that prayer.

I would call each of these prayers "crafted prayers." I didn't start on any of them until I felt God breathing on it. A couple of them were there for months in my heart before anything was written down. I don't feel like these were my idea. I listened and looked for the right words because words have meaning. What I truly feel is these prayers were designed by God in some way to give us a prayer strategy for this hour, which would have lasting Kingdom results. As much as possible, I have referenced at least the chapter where the scriptural truths might be found to support the fact that these are based on biblical truth and not on any man's ideas.

Typically, I would not endorse repeated prayers. Jesus told us not to pray repeated prayers because it often becomes an exercise from rote, and there is no power in just repeating words. However, there are moments and times when we need to get on the same page with God and go in the same direction, in thought, word, and action. I feel very strongly that this is one of those critical times. Having prayers crafted toward specific scriptural outcomes lets us best declare and decree spiritual truth in a focused and strategic way.

I have also found that when this prayer flows in you, and the authorization and some of the terminology gets woven into you, then it is not necessary to work from a crafted prayer every time. The fourth prayer was born in just that way. In a recent Go To Nations board of directors' meeting, I felt like I should pray for one of our businessmen, who is on the cusp of a major venture breakthrough. As I declared and decreed scriptural promises over the venture, I heard words that were not in my normal prayer language, and I knew we needed a crafted prayer for business owners.

Words mean something. They paint pictures. They create and recreate atmospheres. "All that is" exists because of words spoken by God and carried by the very breath of God, the Holy Spirit. Timothy says all Scripture is God-breathed. When God breathes, what comes out? Holy

Spirit! In the Old Testament, the "breath" of God and the "Spirit" of God are the same word—*ruach* in Hebrew. We need Heaven-inspired terminology that agrees with the mind and will of Heaven to see Kingdom results.

You can pray the prayers just as they are. As global organizations, Go To Nations and GloDev, our Relief and Development Arm, we desire greatly to be aligned with God and where He is going in this season to see the global impact we were created for. Your prayers of agreement can move us toward that.

Also, you can simply change the name of our organization to your organization, ministry, or business, where it is relevant in each of these prayers, and begin to speak them over your current and coming season. Another thing you can do is break out parts of these prayers that apply to finances, family, ministry, and so on. There are parts of these prayers that might best fit the season you are in. Use those decrees and declarations that apply God's Word and His will to your situation. I have a friend who works for a very large high school in our area, and he was facing some real challenges with the team in his department. I shared some of these truths with him and encouraged him that he had authority to bind, to loose, to declare and decree. The next time I saw him, he told me things had completely changed. Governmental anointing will move it, and governmental favor will surround it.

This was certainly a divinely inspired project for me, and I give God glory for what is on these pages. I humbly acknowledge that I became the "pen of a ready writer" in this process, yielding to what I believe is a desire, even a mandate from Heaven for His church in this hour. Having said that, I encourage you that the same Holy Spirit could easily take the truth you gain in this reading, and the inspiration of the prayers in the rest of this book, to have you craft your divinely inspired targeted prayers. Jesus always asked those in need "what they wanted" from Him before He prayed. For prayers to hit the mark, the target needs to be defined. Be specific. If these prayers become a catalyst for you by creating effective prayers, then how much more of the will of Heaven would be spoken into the earth? James 5:16 says, "The effective (fervent) prayer of a righteous man can accomplish much."

So make these a part of your daily prayer life. I keep them in the Notes App on my phone, so I always have them available and have used them in specific meetings and services as the Lord directs. The key to prayer is *prayer*. It is not what we know, but what we **do**. Find ways to establish declarative governmental prayer over your current and coming season, our nation, the nations, and those God is using to finance Kingdom ventures globally.

Also, I have provided a list of apostolic prayers, prayers voiced by the apostles in the New Testament. These are powerful prayers that fit specific situations at strategic times. Use them.

Finally, at the back of this book are a few recommended books that have been instrumental in providing truth I currently carry, which I believe will help anyone seeking to go deeper and see greater effectiveness in spiritual authority and targeted prayer.

We entrust these to you as tools to pray for Go To Nations, GloDev, (*your ministry or business*), the government of the United States of America, or the nation you are petitioning God for. God's Word "accomplishes what He sent it to do" (Isa. 55:11).

It is time for the body of Christ to permeate, saturate, and penetrate the atmosphere of Earth, by declaring and decreeing God's Word over, above, before, around, through, and instead of every situation "that exalts itself against the knowledge of God" (2 Cor. 10:5). Because "Worthy is the Lamb that was slain to receive *power*, and *riches*, and *wisdom*, and *strength*, and *honor*, and *glory*, and *blessing*" (Rev. 5:12).

I believe we are in a divine hour. There may never be another moment like this in our lifetimes. What we do in this season will impact our future one way or another. Let's declare and decree God's word and God's will as we are authorized to do so.

10

PREPARING THE SOIL

The first item of *Kingdom business* in this book is a Prayer of Repentance and Agreement. Psalm 24:3–4 says, "Who shall ascend unto the hill of the Lord? Or stand in his Holy Place? He that has clean hands and a pure heart." If we are going to operate from our seated heavenly position (Eph. 2:6), authorized in kingly, governmental, and apostolic intercession, we have to come in clean.

As 2 Chronicles 7:14 says, "If my people…humble themselves and pray, turning from their wicked ways…then I will…" **If we will, He will!** It is always like that.

1 Peter 4:7 says, "Judgement must begin in the house of God." Authority in prayer starts with us being right-minded, right-hearted, and right-

positioned with God, allowing our Father, brother, and Holy Spirit to search and cleanse us.

Identification and repentance prayers have been actively used nationally and globally and have no doubt set the stage for the hour we are now entering. I believe those types of prayers will continue as specific revelation is unveiled or made known. *Repentance prayer rightly readies an altar where declarative and petitioning prayer is the most effective.*

11

PRAYER OF REPENTANCE
AND AGREEMENT

Father, You said in Your Word that our salvation is in repentance and rest, our strength is in quietness and trust (Isa. 30:5).

You say in Your Word that judgment begins with the Lord's household (1 Pet. 4:17).

And You tell us that if Your people who are called by Your name, will humble themselves and pray and seek Your face and turn from their wicked ways; then You will hear from Heaven, forgive our sins, and heal our land (2 Chron. 7:14).

Father, we declare today that we agree with Your Word (Amos 3:3; Matt. 18:19).

Father, we humble ourselves and confess that we have trusted ourselves instead of You. We have trusted our government officials instead of You. We have trusted our abilities, our plans, our purposes instead of You. For this, we repent and ask Your forgiveness.

Father, we humble ourselves and confess that we have not always obeyed Your word to "be not conformed to this world but to be transformed by renewing our minds, proving the will of God, that which is good and acceptable and perfect" (Rom. 12:2). We have weakened and compromised Your word out of fear, fear of man, unbelief, and pride. For this, we repent and ask Your forgiveness.

Father, we humble ourselves and confess that we have allowed the longings of our flesh, the longings of our eyes, and the arrogance of life to rule our thoughts, our actions, our activities, and our pursuits. We have not sought first the Kingdom of Heaven as You instruct us, and we have not trusted You in all things or entrusted You with all things. For this, we repent and ask Your forgiveness.

Forgive us, Father, for building our own kingdoms and protecting our own names instead of stewarding Your Kingdom and exalting **Your** name.

Forgive us, Father, for those who are **still** yet to be reached with the good news of Christ in nations and places where we have not gone personally or sent someone in our place (Rom 10:13–15).

Forgive us, Father, for those who remain the objects of prejudice and discrimination where we have not taken Christ and been a voice of healing and restoration.

Forgive us, Father, for those who are tortured and persecuted for their profession of Christ while we have remained silent on Your behalf.

Forgive us, Father, for those who are victims of human trafficking, slavery, and social injustice while we remain busy with other things and unmoved by their plight.

Forgive us, Father, for lacking the courage to accept and obey the great commandments of the New Testament to love God with all of our hearts, our souls, our minds, and our strength; to love our neighbors as ourselves; and to go and make disciples of all nations (Mark 12:30–31; Matt. 28:19).

Father, judge our hearts in this hour. As we humble ourselves, bring us to a place of brokenness and contrition for what we have allowed to remain that is a compromised version of You or Your Word in any way.

Teach us to seek Your face as never before. You tell us in Your Word that Your eyes are searching the earth to find those whose hearts are fully committed to You so that You can show Yourself strong on their behalf (2 Chron. 16:9). May we be those people, Lord.

As we turn toward You, forgive us, Lord, forgive our nation, forgive Your Church, Lord, forgive Your shepherds; Father, forgive those who claim to speak on Your behalf but miss or misrepresent the heart of God.

Forgive us for not "honoring all" of Your creation as You direct in Your Word (1 Pet. 2:17).

You tell us that mercy triumphs over judgment (James 2:13).

Be merciful, Lord, as we rend our hearts, release grace as we come to You in repentance (Joel 2:13).

Show us the ancient paths that we may walk in that which is good (Jer. 6:16).

Exalt Your highways of holiness, Lord (Isa. 49:11).

Lead us in the way of righteousness (Prov. 8:20).

Teach us Your ways, Lord, that we may walk in Your paths, so that Your Word may go forth and have free course (Mic. 4:2; 2 Thess. 3:1).

Fill us once again with power from on high, to be Your witnesses at home, in our cities and neighborhoods, our churches and businesses, our states, our nation, and to the very ends of the earth (Acts 1:8).

Yours, and Yours alone, is the Kingdom, and the power, and the glory, forever (Matt. 6:13).

Amen

12

MINISTRY DECLARATION
INTRODUCTION

This first prayer was the first declarative/governmental prayer I wrote late in 2015. It is the broadest and speaks the most to whom we are as believers in Christ and what God says about us. It speaks to our mandate and agreement with God's Word. This prayer speaks prophetically to the future as we see it set before us.

Also, this prayer speaks to our families, children, and grandchildren, calling all of these things into alignment with what Scripture declares to be true. And it is in this prayer that we first express what I call "governmental anointing" based on the revelation of Isaiah 45 and several of the Scriptures that are foundational for this type of prayer.

This is the prayer we have been praying the longest and therefore have seen the most fruit from. Many of us are seeing breakthrough in finances, spiritual breakthrough in family members, new doors opening for ministry and relationships, and old doors closing that were hindering or limiting what God desired to do. We are seeing alignment and realignment at an unprecedented rate. Where we used to see shifts in our ministry every three to five years, we are seeing major movement in literally months now. *Repeatedly*. This is a faith-filled overcomer's strategic prayer that we are seeing change some very difficult environments and help us navigate uncharted waters as never before.

It is through this prayer that things beyond our natural control, even at a civil, local, or national government level, have shifted in favor of God's Kingdom, with a residual release of governmental favor.

13

MINISTRY DECLARATION

Father, we proclaim that Go To Nations, GloDev, or *(your ministry)* is Your idea.

This ministry was born in the heart of God and carries divine design and spiritual DNA for the nations: God's **D**estiny, Christ **N**ature, and Holy Spirit **A**nointing (Col. 1; 1 Pet. 1; Rom. 8; Eph. 1).

We understand that Your eyes are on the nations, and as Your sons and daughters, You authorize us to claim what is rightfully Yours as our inheritance on Your behalf (Ps. 2; John 16; Rom. 8; Rev. 2).

We acknowledge that every man, woman, child, father, mother, sister, brother, son, and daughter in each nation is the prize, passion, and pursuit of Your heart (2 Pet. 2; John 3; Luke 19).

We declare and decree that we are partakers of **that** divine nature and stewards of **those** Kingdom purposes revealed to us, proclaimed by us, and demonstrated and fulfilled through us on Earth (1 Pet. 1, 4; 1 Cor. 2, 4; 1 John 1)

We declare and decree that whatever is born of God overcomes in this world. Therefore, every member of Go To Nations, GloDev or (*your ministry*) is permeated, saturated, endued, and empowered with an overcoming Spirit. The Holy Spirit in us does not let up, give up, lighten up, or shut up until we have fulfilled God's purpose in us for our generation (1 John 5; Acts 1; Rom. 8, 15; 1 Cor. 2, 12; Rev. 2; Heb. 9; Eph. 3).

We declare and decree that You go before us to level the mountains and make the crooked places straight. We shout grace, grace to every mountain. We shout grace, grace to every mountain (Luke 3; Isa. 40; Zech. 4).

We declare and decree that You will break down the gates of bronze and cut through bars of iron that hinder Your purposes in any way. Your Word accomplishes what You sent it to do. Your Word has free course. Your Word does not fail. Your Word endures forever (Isa. 45, 55; Ps. 119; 1 Pet. 1; Heb. 1; 2 Thess. 3).

We declare and decree that signs and wonders **will** accompany the preaching of Your Word, and we will see the miraculous in increasing measure. Your anointing in us will break every yoke. Your power will fill us and flow through us (Acts 1, 14; Heb. 2; John 14; Isa. 10).

We declare and decree that You give us the treasures of darkness hidden in the secret places (Isa. 45).

We declare and decree that God always causes us to triumph in Christ Jesus.

Therefore, we are ministers marked by triumph, champions declaring and decreeing the goodness of God, carrying light and life to the nations (2 Cor. 2; Rom. 2, 8; Jer. 20; 1 John 1; 1 Pet. 2; Ps. 23, 27; Gal. 2)

We declare and decree that we are filled with the Spirit of revelation, the Spirit of wisdom and understanding, the Spirit of counsel and might, the Spirit of knowledge, and the fear of the Lord (Rev. 1; Isa. 11; Eph. 1, 3; Gal. 1).

We declare and decree that Jesus is made unto us wisdom in every circumstance.

We declare and decree that together we have the mind of Christ on all matters. (1 Cor. 1, 2; Eph. 1)

We declare and decree that we are thoroughly, fully, totally, and completely equipped for every good work (2 Tim. 3).

We declare and decree that **we have** the *maps* of Heaven's direction. We declare and decree that **we have** the *blueprints* of divine strategies. We declare and decree that **we have** the *keys* of Kingdom authority to open doors in every nation that no man can shut and to shut doors that no man can open, to bind every work of darkness and to loose the will of Heaven on the earth (Gen. 1; Ps. 33; Prov. 16; Jer. 29; Isa. 22; Matt. 16).

We declare and decree that You, Father, are Creator of all that exist and You, Jesus, have redeemed this world by Your blood. We are twice owned by You.

We declare and decree that You have set Your throne in the heavens and Your Kingdom rules over all. The Earth is the Lord's and all who dwell in it (Col. 1; Isa. 40; Gen. 1; Gal. 3; 1 Pet. 1; Ps. 24, 93, 103; 1 Cor.10).

We declare and decree that as high King of Heaven, righteous judge of creation, Lord of all and supreme authority, "the courtroom of Heaven" is the final word on every matter, in every nation, under every government, every single time (Ps. 47, 119, 138; Dan. 4; 2 Tim. 4; Zech. 6; Matt. 28; Isa. 55; Phil. 2).

We declare and decree that Your Kingdom will come and Your will shall be done in all that concerns us and You—today, tomorrow, and every day after that (Matt. 6; Luke 11; Isa. 40, 55; Heb. 13).

We declare and decree that as King, You execute judgment and divine justice in situations that grieve Your heart, according to Your unending mercy, Your unfailing righteousness, and Your unfathomable love (1 Tim. 6; Rev. 17, 19; Ps. 9; 2 Tim. 4; James 2, 5; 1 John 2; 1 Cor. 13).

We declare and decree that as we walk in obedience to You, we are blessed in the cities where we live and in the countries where we go; we are blessed when we come in, we are blessed when we go out (Deut. 28).

We declare and decree that in every situation, we are the head and not the tail; we are above and not beneath (Deut. 28).

We declare and decree that whatever we put our hands to prospers; we are the lenders and not borrowers (Deut. 28).

We declare and decree that we are the seed of Abraham and through Your covenant we are blessed to be a blessing to all families on the face of the earth (Gal. 3, 4; Gen. 12; Deut. 8).

We declare and decree that You give us the ability to create wealth in order to establish Your "covenant of blessing" to all people (Deut. 8).

We declare and decree all that has been stolen from us personally or as a ministry—physically, spiritually, financially, or relationally—shall be repaid (Prov. 6; Exod. 22).

We declare and decree that You desire above all things that we prosper and be in good health, even as our souls prosper. We are the healed of the Lord (3 John 2; Jer. 17).

We declare and decree that our souls are prospering, our families are prospering, our ministries are prospering, our marriages are prospering, our teams are prospering, our finances are prospering, and our health is prospering (Ps. 1, 67; 3 John 2; Zech. 8; Josh. 1; 1 John 5; Prov. 10).

We declare and decree that we are prosperous and debt free. We speak jubilee to our season (Lev. 25; Deut. 28; Rom. 13; Ps. 25, 37; Prov. 21).

We declare and decree that no weapon dreamed, schemed, fashioned, or formed against us prospers (Isa. 54).

We declare and decree that we are surrounded with goodness, favor, and the all-sufficiency of grace that in all things, at all times, we have all that we need (Rom. 15; Ps. 5, 23, 27, 84, 90; 2 Cor. 6, 8, 9, 12; 1 Cor.15; Eph. 1).

We declare and decree that our children and our children's children will walk in a full revelation of their spiritual inheritance as our sons and daughters and Yours (Ezek. 37; Ps. 103, 105; Gen. 9, 45, 48; Deut. 7; Isa. 44, 54, 59, 61; Jer. 31; Dan. 4; Luke 1).

We declare and decree that our descendants shall possess the gates and cities of their enemies; our children will be mighty in the land (Gen. 24; Isa. 54; Ps. 112).

We declare and decree that You number our days, that our times and seasons are in Your hands, as our days are, so shall our strength be, and we shall live long in the earth and the nations You give to us (Prov. 3; Deut. 33; Ps. 31, 37, 90, 139; Jer. 35; Isa. 40, 65).

We declare and decree that the earth shall be filled with the knowledge of the glory of the Lord as the waters cover the sea (Hab. 2).

We declare and decree there shall be no repercussions, retribution, or retaliation against us, our children, our children's children, or this ministry in Jesus's name (Isa. 54:17; Matt. 16:19; Ps. 91).

Yours is the Kingdom and the power and the glory forever. Amen.

14

GOVERNMENT DECLARATION
INTRODUCTION

During the 2016 elections, I felt a strong burden to take up a more biblical prayer strategy for our government and leaders as well, all based on Scripture. As the Lord has drawn me deeper into understanding prayer authorized at this level, He has continued to reveal more understanding. As the 2016 presidential elections drew closer, I had a strong sense of the outcome and was mindful of a few things taking place that seemed to confirm what I was feeling.

I signed up for early morning prayer at our church on the Monday before the election and the Tuesday morning of the election. I went to the church prayer room early in the morning to pray and met with God. As I was petitioning and declaring truth over the election and its outcome, I sensed the strong presence of the Lord. As my prayer time came to an end, I simply heard the Lord say, "I've got this Craig. It is not by might, nor by power, but by my Spirit" (Zech. 4:6).

I knew at that point it was in His hands. I rarely stay up to watch election results, but I was captured late in the evening as the tide began to turn and the impossible became possible. But then the Lord spoke again and said, "Craig, this election was not the end; it was only the beginning. **Now** is the time to pray." I knew at that point we needed to cover our elected president, the newly forming cabinet, and the government of our nation with greater prayer. I also felt I was being authorized to go after the mountains or domains of influence that have so taken our nation and much of the world captive.

This prayer speaks to those mountains. I strongly recommend Pastor Johnny Enlow's book *The Seven Mountain Prophecy* for insight and understanding in this area. Isaiah 2:2 says, "in the last days, the mountain of the Lord's house (the New Testament Church) shall be established on the top of all other mountains."

This prayer is full of Scripture that speaks to the nations God blesses and the results of those blessings, decreeing and calling this nation, or any other, back into alignment with Heaven. It also speaks to some of our current and recent social, cultural, and national issues where God desires to show Himself strong.

This prayer can be used for other nations or governments by simply changing some of the specifics, while leaving much of the rest as it is.

15

GOVERNMENT/NATIONAL DECLARATION

Father, we declare and decree that You have set Your throne in the heavens and Your Kingdom rules over all (Ps. 103:19).

The Earth is the Lord's and those who dwell in it (Ps. 24:1).

We declare and decree that "blessed is the nation whose God is the Lord" (Ps. 33:12). We are a blessed nation, and in this unfolding season we are going to see the blessing of the Lord return to our government, our leaders, our businesses, our churches, our towns and cities, and the mountains of influence.

Father, we thank You that You have heard our prayers as a nation. We acknowledge that it is by Your mercy that we have been saved as a nation and positioned for a season of victory and increase (Prov. 21:31).

We declare and decree today that You lead victory to justice and we shall (again) be a nation of liberty and justice for all (Matt. 12:20).

We declare that when the righteous prosper, the city rejoices (Prov. 11:10).

We declare that righteous rules, laws, ordinances, judgments, and justice shall return to our judicial system, and our nation, and that righteousness shall prosper.

We declare and decree today that all blessing, glory, wisdom, thanksgiving, honor, power, and might belong to You forever and ever (Rev. 7:12).

Father, Your Word tells us in 1 Timothy 2:1 that "first of all petitions, prayers, intercession, and thanksgiving be made for all people."

Father, we pray for our neighbors, our coworkers, our communities, our towns, and cities today that Your Kingdom would come. Your will would be done in greater measure (Matt. 6:10).

That as a nation, the eyes of our understanding would be opened that we might know the hope of Your calling (Eph. 1:8).

Father, Your Word continues in 1 Timothy 2:2 that "petitions, prayers, intercession, and thanksgiving be made for kings and all those in authority, that we may live peaceful and quiet lives in all godliness and holiness."

We declare and decree that promotion does not come from the East or from the West, but You set one in place and take another one down (Ps. 75:6).

So we lift up our newly elected president, his wife, his sons and daughters, and his grandchildren.

We lift up our vice president, his wife, and his children.

We pray the hand of the Lord would surround them and go before them (Ps. 5; Isa. 45).

We set angels and a hedge of protection about them to keep them safe and deliver them from evil (Job 1:10; Matt. 6:13).

We declare that no weapon dreamed, schemed, fashioned, or formed against them shall prosper (Isa. 54:17).

We declare that no calamity shall befall them (Jon. 4:2).

We declare that any plot or plan of the enemy that would bring harm in any way would be exposed and stopped in Jesus's name (Dan. 2; 1 Cor. 4:5; Ps. 91).

We declare and decree that our president, his advisers, his cabinet, and national leadership team shall be filled with the Spirit of revelation, the

Spirit of wisdom and understanding, the Spirit of counsel and might, the Spirit of knowledge, and the fear of the Lord (Isa. 11:2).

We declare and decree that You are our peace and You have destroyed the barrier, the dividing wall of hostility (Eph. 2:14).

We declare and decree today that it is not by might, it is not by power, but it is by Your Spirit. And we speak to every mountain in this nation, saying, "You shall become a plain." We speak grace, grace to every mountain (Zech. 4:6–7).

We speak peace to every racial barrier in our nation and pull them down (Eph. 2).

We speak peace to every spiritual barrier in our nation and pull them down (Eph. 2).

We speak peace to every gender barrier in our nation and pull them down (Eph. 2).

We speak peace to every cultural barrier in our nation and pull them down (Eph. 2).

We speak peace to every political barrier in our nation and pull them down (Eph. 2).

We speak peace to every class barrier in our nation and pull them down (Eph. 2).

We declare and decree today that there shall be peace within our walls, and prosperity within our citadels, strongholds, and fortresses (Ps. 122:7).

We declare and decree today that our founding cry was "one nation under God," and under God, we shall (again) be one nation (John 17; Eph. 2).

We declare and decree today that the weapons of our warfare are not of this world, but they have divine power to demolish strongholds (2 Cor. 10:4).

We declare and decree today that whatever is born of God overcomes in this world (1 John 5:4).

We declare and decree today that You have given us the keys of the Kingdom, keys of governmental, apostolic, and spiritual authority, and with those keys, whatever we bind on Earth has already been bound in Heaven (Isa. 22:22; Matt. 16:19).

We declare and decree today that every mountain shall become plain, clear, obvious, and transparent to Your people (Isa. 48:6).

So with the authority of Heaven, in the name of Jesus, the name that is above every name (Phil. 2:9), we bind up the spirit of pride, corruption, deception, manipulation, and fear at work in the mountain of government. We release the power of God to be at work in the executive branch, the legislative branch, and the judicial branch of our government. We release divine supernatural wisdom to figure out the difficult issues. We release the Spirit of revelation to be at work. We release the spirit of Nehemiah to rebuild the spiritual walls of our nation (Isa. 58; Matt. 16).

We bind up the spirit of the destroyer who works through the mountain of media to disperse bad news and promote fear and mistrust. We stop distortion, lies, and deception in the name of Jesus. We release the blessing of God, the good news to fill our national media outlets. We declare and decree that **truth** will prevail in this nation, and truth will bring true freedom (Matt. 16; John 8:32; Jer. 27).

In the name of Jesus, we bind up the spirit of humanism, deception, and pride at work in the mountain of education. We release the Spirit of wisdom, understanding, revelation, and humility in its place. We release the Spirit of divine counsel. We call for a return to the ancient paths of biblical truth, knowledge, and spiritual foundations that God would be enthroned on the mountain of education. We declare and decree a holy redemption of the values and ethics in our educational system. We release a supernatural movement that brings strength, alignment, renewal, and restoration of kingdom principles that again pass spiritual inheritance from generation to generation (Matt. 16; Isa. 11).

We bind up the spirit of greed, control, deception, and manipulation that works through the mountain of economy. We release in its place the Spirit of understanding of true riches, the Spirit of humility, and service (Matt. 16; Prov. 22; Gen. 12; Deut. 8).

In the name of Jesus, we bind up the spirit of pride, seduction, compromise, and perversion that works through the mountain of the arts in this nation. We release in its place the glory of the Kingdom. We release a Spirit of righteousness and peace over performers, entertainers, and industry leaders (Matt. 16; Ps. 29; Hab. 2).

In the name of Jesus, we bind up the spirit of idolatry, pride, fear, contention, and perversion that works through the mountain of religion. We bind the orphan spirit, the spirit of slavery, and pride. In its place, we release the Spirit of sonship, righteousness, honor, and the fear of the Lord. We call the New Testament church, the *ekklesia*, into her ordained place as the governing, legislative assembly of the saints from Matthew 16:18–19. We say, "Arise church, and take your stand—united and unashamed, faithful and fearless, blood bought and bold, holy and wholly committed to finish the task, without spot, wrinkle, or blemish. We declare and decree a New Testament church that operates fully in its purpose, position, and role. We release a supernatural movement that brings holy inspiration, divine integration, spiritual transformation, and generational impartation that will influence and impact all other mountains for the Kingdom of God" (Matt. 16; 1 Pet. 2; Heb. 2; 2 Chron. 19).

We bind the spirit of rejection, perversion, and the orphan spirit of Baal that works in the mountain of family. We release in its place the Spirit of adoption, the Spirit of understanding, and the Spirit of might. We call for a return to the ancient paths of marriage, as a holy spiritual union between one man and one woman. We call forth godly husbands and wives who honor the sanctity of marriage. We declare and decree that God-ordained biblical marriages shall be recognized, valued, and honored in our nation. We call into place godly mothers, fathers, sons, daughters, and families. We declare and decree a holy redemption of biblical family values that have been lost, stolen, or neglected. We release a supernatural movement that brings strength, alignment, renewal, and restoration of the patriarchal and matriarchal spirits that again pass spiritual inheritance from generation to generation (Matt. 16; Rom. 8; Isa. 11).

We declare and decree that the mountain of the Lord's house, the Church, is being exalted and established over all other mountains; that the name of Jesus is the Name above every other name; that **every** knee, **every** name must bow to that name (Isa. 2:2; Ps. 148:13; Eph. 1:21; Phil. 2:9).

Father, we declare and decree that we are in an Isaiah 45 season. You have established and anointed this administration as a Cyrus government to realign this nation with Your plans and purposes (Isa. 45:1; Ps. 33).

We declare and decree that You are shattering the doors of bronze and cutting through bars of iron that hold this government, the church, this nation, and our families in bondage in this hour (Isa. 45:2).

We declare and decree that You will give us the treasures of darkness hidden in these mountains, hidden in the secret places in this hour (Isa. 45:3). That wisdom from above is being released to see, hear, and understand the challenges and solutions for this hour (Matt. 13:6).

We declare and decree Revelation 5:12: "Worthy is the Lamb that was slain to receive *power*, and *riches*, and *wisdom*, and *strength*, and *honor*, and *glory*, and *blessing*."

We declare and decree Isaiah 11:2 that the sevenfold Spirit of the Lord shall be made manifest in these mountains and the Spirit of divine revelation shall release the Spirit of wisdom and understanding; the Spirit of counsel and might; the Spirit of knowledge; and the fear of the Lord, over, in, and through these mountains, our president, the cabinet, his advisers, and Your church in this nation.

We declare and decree there shall be no repercussions, retribution, or retaliation against us, our children, our children's children, or this ministry, in Jesus's name (Isa. 54:17; Matt. 16:19; Ps. 91).

Yours is the Kingdom and the power and the glory forever. Amen.

16

NATIONS' DECLARATION
INTRODUCTION

This prayer is a passionate and powerful declaration of God's heart and ours for the nations, resonating with the power of divine agreement, supernatural expectation, and the authority of sonship to both dispossess and possess nations.

It declares God's rightful position over the nations of the earth and decrees our own obedience to the mandate of global missions. In obedience to Scripture, this is a strong call for the next generation of harvesters and laborers to arise, especially in the nations of the world we are reaching and among the now emerging millennial generation. Along with the labor force, there must be financial resource. Please say that again. Along with the labor force, there must be financial resource. A significant focus of this prayer then is on the economic engine that empowers global missions.

As Psalm 2 declares, "Ask of me and I will give you the nations as your inheritance, the ends of the earth as your possession." But as I explained in chapter 3, "Claiming Inheritance," the "ask" is only one side of inheritance. The other side is Matthew 28, where we are commanded to "go." Romans 10:13–15 ties all of this together, saying, "How can they believe if they have not heard, and how can they hear if someone does not preach? And how can they preach unless they are sent?"

I have gotten off planes for twenty-seven years in Asia and asked taxi drivers if they know Jesus. Most have **never** ever heard the name. Whatever their current religion, they don't even know they have a choice because they have never been told. How can they believe unless someone shares or preaches? Our director in Thailand calls it "an unequal distribution of the Gospel." Much of the world has little or no distribution. When we started in Thailand, there was one church per fifty thousand people.

There must be a "goer" to claim inheritance and make disciples. For there to be a goer, there must be a "sender." Romans is very clear on this. Any targeted prayer strategy for nations has to include not only the nation or people group we are focused on but also the goers, the laborers Jesus talks about, and the senders Romans calls for to make that happen. This prayer speaks forth and calls all of this into place.

17

NATIONS' DECLARATION

Father, as in all things, we declare Your Lordship. You—You—You have set Your throne in the heavens and Your Kingdom rules over all. You are not shaken. You do not waiver. You are steadfast, immovable, always faithful, and without shadow (Ps. 24, 103; Heb. 13).

We declare and decree that from the beginning, before even one fragment of life existed on this earth, Your eyes were on the nations. We see in Your Word that every man, woman, child, father, mother, sister, and brother are the prize, passion, and pursuit of Your heart (2 Pet. 3).

Your "love without limits" displayed on the cross opens the way for all who would receive. You say in Your Word, "How can they believe in one of whom they have not heard? How can they hear unless someone preach? How can they preach, unless they are sent?" (Rom. 10).

Father, we proclaim and testify that we are Your sent ones. We have heard Your clarion call to go, to reach, to preach, to teach. We proclaim that Your mission is our mission. Every member of Go To Nations has given themselves in obedience to the mission of the church, the Great Commission (Matt. 28; 2 Cor. 5; Mark 16; John 17; Acts 1).

Father, according to Your Word, as we walk in obedience to You, Your blessings come upon us and overtake us. We are the blessed of the Lord. As Your covenant children, we declare that we are blessed to be a blessing to **all** nations on the face of the earth (Deut. 28; Gen. 12).

Father, we declare that we are in a Cyrus season, a season where Your hand is on global leaders in a fresh and tangible way to proclaim peace to the nations. You are assembling an army of believers to lift high Your banner, to lift high Your name, to lift one another, and to lift the lost on every continent. We call into place, into rank, into order, into alignment every man, woman, and child whom You have ordained to be a part of this company (Isa. 45; Deut. 20; John 12; Joel 2).

We speak to the valleys of dry bones all over this earth today: We say to the nations of the North, the South, the East and the West, "Arise! Arise! Arise!" We release the *ruach*, the breath, the Spirit of the living God, and we prophesy life to dry bones and those whose vision and calling have been slain by the devourer. We declare and decree—come to life! We declare and decree, along with the Lord of the Harvest, that an army of laborers shall come forth in this hour in ranks, in ranks, in ranks. Lifted and established into calling (Ezek. 37).

We declare and decree the release of the spirit of Bezalel to build wisely and skillfully in the nations as God directs (Exod. 36).

We declare and decree the release of the spirit of Ezra and Nehemiah to rebuild the walls around those things You are establishing in the nations (Neh. 2).

We declare that Judah (praise) shall go first (Num. 2:9; Judg. 20:18).

We declare that Judah (praise) plows (Hosea 10:11).

We call forth Levites, true worshippers, to open the heavens over dark places (Isa. 64; John 1, 4).

We stop all distraction, all complacency, all procrastination in Jesus's name. We speak the urgency of the hour into those hearts and minds that You are calling, seeding, sending, and setting into place with Go To Nations, GloDev, or *(your ministry)*. We fill the atmosphere with anticipation surrounding our staff and our world headquarters for planning and releasing of this ministry (Matt. 16; Rom. 8; Phil. 1:20).

We declare we are expectant. Our eyes are fixed on You. It all belongs to You.

We declare Holy Spirit language, Holy Spirit breath, Holy Spirit life, and Holy Spirit lift over every word, every document, every note, every moment of planning and implementation. May You be glorified. May You be lifted. You said, "If I be lifted up, I will draw all men to me." So be it, Lord. So be it, Lord (Heb. 12; Ps. 141; Gen. 14; John 12).

We release divine partnership into the hearts of those whom You are drawing. We release divine entrepreneurship into the hearts of those You are drawing. We release divine financial creativity into the hearts of those You are drawing. We release divine generosity into the hearts of those You are drawing (Deut. 28; 2 Cor. 8, 9; Philem. 6)

We remove financial and spiritual blinders from eyes (2 Cor. 4). We break fear of lack off of every individual (Ps. 34; Phil. 4).

Father, we break the orphan spirit off of this ministry, our leaders, our missionaries, our board members, and our financial partners. No more will we operate from a place of insufficiency for **You** are the all sufficient one (Rom. 8; Ps. 84; 2 Cor. 12).

You said in Your Word, "He who did not spare His own son, but gave Him up for us all, how will He not also along with Him freely give us all things?" We declare and decree that, in a Cyrus season, gates of bronze and bars of iron are obliterated and every chain of financial limitation are removed (Rom. 8; Isa. 45).

We declare and decree the Spirit of adoption, the Spirit of sonship, over this ministry and our financial partners (Rom. 8).

Because we are Your sons and daughters, we are authorized (Rev. 2).

Because we act on Your behalf and not our own, we authorize an unprecedented level of partnership through financial and ministry synergy. We unlock financial freedom.

We declare and decree a **now** season of abundant flow in manpower and resources (Heb. 11; 2 Cor. 5; Luke 10).

We declare and decree a **now** season of pressed down, shaken together, and running over shall men give to airlift the Gospel to the nations (Luke 6).

We declare and decree the realization, formation, and materialization of a great financial company that shall come up under Go To Nations, GloDev, or (*your ministry*) to lift her to new heights of financial strength.

We declare and decree Kingdom alignment for Kingdom assignments.

We declare and decree Kingdom provision for Kingdom reasons in Jesus's name.

We call in partners, new partners, businesses, organizations, grants, inheritance, endowments, wills, trusts, faith promise giving, entrepreneurs, generational wealth, and provision.

We declare and decree Revelation 5:12, "Worthy is the Lamb that was slain to receive *power*, and *riches*, and *wisdom*, and *strength*, and *honor*, and *glory*, and *blessing*."

We declare and decree Isaiah 11:2, "And the Spirit of the Lord shall rest on him (us), the Spirit of wisdom and understanding, the Spirit of counsel and might, the Spirit of knowledge, and of the fear of the Lord."

We declare and decree Deuteronomy 7:1, "The Lord thy God shall bring you into a land to possess it, and cast out many nations before thee, the Hittites, the Girgashites, the Amorites, the Canaanites, the Perizzites, the Hivites, and the Jebusites, seven nations mightier than thee."

We declare and decree that the mountain of the Lord's house, the Church, is being exalted and established over all other mountains; that the name of Jesus is the name above every other name; and that **every** knee, **every** name must bow to that name (Isa. 2:2; Ps. 148:13; Eph. 1:21; Phil. 2:9).

We declare and decree that this is Your day, this is Your time, this is Your season (Ezek. 39; 1 Sam. 24; 2 Cor. 6).

We declare and decree that the earth shall be filled with the knowledge of the glory of the Lord as the waters cover the sea (Hab. 2:14).

We declare and decree that as Your vessel, Go To Nations, GloDev, or (*your ministry*), will be lifted to new heights of financial liberty, ability, and abundance so that Your word may come to pass. In Jesus's name! Amen and amen.

We declare and decree there shall be no repercussions, retribution, or retaliation against us, our children, our children's children, or this ministry and its partners in Jesus's name (Isa. 54:17; Matt. 16:19; Ps. 91).

Yours is the Kingdom and the power and the glory forever. Amen.

18

KINGDOM BUSINESS
DECLARATION INTRODUCTION

Starting at Creation, before the curse, Adam was given the task of tending the Garden. The original mandate to "fill the earth and subdue it" is as much a call to global entrepreneurship as it is evangelism. Throughout the Old Testament, the stories give us a very clear picture of the size and scope of the commerce the patriarchs were involved in. Abraham once amassed an army just from those he employed.

Abraham and Lot had so much wealth they had to expand the territory they covered just to have room. In Genesis 12:1–4, God told Abraham He would bless him, and he (Abraham) would be so blessed all of the families of the earth would be blessed through that blessing. We know that is a spiritual blessing, but also it carried the economic blessing of entrepreneurship that would make it possible.

Then, in Deuteronomy 8:18, we are told that God gives us the ability to create wealth in order to confirm His covenant. This verse clearly refers to the "blessed to bless" covenant God made with Abraham. God intends both Kingdom message (the Gospel) and Kingdom resource (the road that carries it) to flow together.

In the New Testament book of Acts, most of the early spiritual encounters took place in the marketplace. We see written down these descriptions, "Simon the tanner" and "Lydia, the seller of purple." Why do we care what their professions were? We care because God cared enough to get it in the story! God wants us to know that he works as much in the marketplace as he does in the sanctuary. More actually, as was demonstrated in the book of Acts.

It is time to stop calling anointed men and women out of the marketplace and to release them into global entrepreneurship to change economic systems. That will bless nations, the people of God, and make possible "discipling nations" that Jesus speaks to in Matthew 28.

This prayer is Kingdom authorization for businessmen and women, business owners of every size, financial dreamers, and entrepreneurs. Now is the time to see financial harvest unleashed for the purpose of stockpiling the machinery needed for a global harvest of souls!

19

KINGDOM BUSINESS DECLARATION

Father, we stand in awe of You today. We proclaim as You say in Your Word, "Thine is the Kingdom, and the power, and the glory forever" (Matt. 6:13).

The entire Earth is the Lord's, everything in it and everyone on it (Ps. 24:1).

We proclaim today that You are Creator of all that exist—every mineral, every fiber, every technology, every plant, every chemical; everything we touch, move, envision, develop, or distribute comes from You. You created it all and You own it all. We are here to steward all that is rightfully **Yours** (Gen. 1–3; Col. 1; Acts 17:28).

All power is **Yours**.
All wisdom is **Yours**.

All riches are **Yours.**
All strength is **Yours.**
All honor is **Yours.**
All glory is **Yours.**
All blessing is **Yours** (Rev. 5:12).
It all belongs to You, and You alone.

There is none like You. All that exists is by Your will and by Your Word, spoken into existence. Lord, we acknowledge today that apart from You we can do nothing (Col. 1).

In **You**, we live and move and have our being (Acts 17:28).

It is not in our ability or our strength; it is not by might, nor by power, but by Your Spirit that we are who we are and where we are in this hour (Zech. 4:6).

We declare and decree that You have given us eyes to see, ears to hear, and hearts to know and understand (Deut. 29:4; Isa. 32:4).

We declare and decree that we have the Spirit of revelation, the Spirit of wisdom and understanding, the Spirit of counsel and might, the Spirit of knowledge, and the fear of the Lord at work within us (Isa. 11:2).

We declare and decree that Christ has been made unto us wisdom; that wisdom abides in us, and in wisdom dwells the knowledge of witty inventions (1 Cor. 1:30, Prov. 8:12).

Father, You are the meta-entrepreneur. The first spoken words out of Your mouth were "fill the earth and subdue, bring it under (Kingdom) dominion" (Gen. 1:28).

Every idea born in Your heart and conveyed to ours has potential to shape this entire world and advance Your Kingdom in the earth (1 John 5).

Your covenant with Abraham, the father of us all, is "blessed to be a blessing to all families on the face of the earth" (Gen. 12:1–4).

You said in Deuteronomy 8:18 that You "give us the ability to create wealth and so confirm the covenant" of "blessed to be a blessing."

And You say in Deuteronomy 28 that as we walk in obedience to You, Your blessings come upon us and overtake us.

We declare and decree **today** that we are run down and crushed under the weight of the blessing, provision, goodness, and influence of God (Deut. 28).

You said in 1 John 5, "**Whatever** is born of God, overcomes in this world." So today, Father, we declare that this business, this endeavor, (_____), is born of God. You gave us the design, the blueprints, the keys, the strategies.

So we call into place the will of Heaven for this venture (Deut. 8:18).

We call into place supernatural connection to global movers, shakers, and decision-makers in this industry. And we declare that we have favor with God and favor with man. Even favor with kings and rulers (Luke 2:52; Prov. 14:35; Esther 8:5).

We are financial ambassadors of Heaven, sent ones in the marketplace, apostolic pioneers of Heaven's economics (2 Cor. 5:20; Acts 17:17).

We declare and decree that this company has been brought into the Kingdom for such a time as this (Esther 4:14).

We speak forth open doors over (_____), its officers and leaders that no man can close (Isa. 22:22).

We declare and decree that we have the keys of the Kingdom and whatever we loose on Earth is already loosed in Heaven. We loose supernatural favor, provision, blessing, strategy, and strength over (_____) (Matt. 16:18).

KINGDOM BUSINESS DECLARATION

We declare and decree divine alignment over, in, and through (_____
_____) (Heb. 10:5).

We declare and decree Your Kingdom come. Your Will be done over, in,
and through (_____) (Matt. 6:10).

We declare and decree **rivers** of financial resource moving through
(_____), through our financial officers, into the Kingdom
and the nations (Gen. 2).

We declare and decree that the blessings of the Lord maketh rich and no
sorrow is added to it (Prov. 10:22).

We declare that great wealth is in the house of the righteous (Prov. 15:6).

We declare and decree that we are prospering even as our souls are
prospering (3 John 2).

We declare peace within the walls of (_____) and prosperity
within our dwellings (Ps. 122:7).

We declare and decree that when the righteous prosper the cities rejoice.
(Prov. 11:10).

We declare and decree that **whole cities** will overflow with prosperity (Zech. 1:17).

We declare and decree today that God always causes us to triumph in Christ Jesus (2 Cor. 2:14).

We declare and decree that in **all things** we are **more** than conquerors (Rom. 8:37).

We declare and decree that we are in a Cyrus season (Isa. 45). That You, Lord, go before us to level every mountain, every obstacle that hinders Your plans and purposes. You, Lord, are breaking every bronze gate of impossibility and opposition. You, Lord, are cutting through every iron bar of lack and limitation.

We declare and decree today that **You** bestow favor and honor, and we will never for one moment lack any good thing (Ps. 84:11).

Father, we break the spirit of poverty over our minds and mind-sets and any assignment against (_____) (2 Cor. 10:4).

We break the orphan spirit off of our minds and (_____) and release the spirit of sonship in its place. We declare that we walk in the full rights of sonship (Gal. 4:5; John 1:12).

We declare and decree Isaiah 54:17 that no weapon, dreamed, schemed, fashioned, or formed against this company or any of its officers and officials, shall prosper.

We declare and decree that the mountain of the Lord's house, the Church, is being exalted and established over all other mountains; that the name of Jesus is the name above every other name; that **every** knee, **every** name must bow to that name (Isa. 2:2; Ps. 148:13; Eph. 1:21; Phil. 2:9).

We declare and decree that our storehouse, our accounts, our repositories shall constantly be filled with every kind of provision and that our goods and products will increase by thousands and by tens of thousands where we are sowing seed (Ps. 144:13).

We declare and decree there shall be no repercussions, retribution, or retaliation against us, our children, our children's children or this business, in Jesus's name (Matt. 16:19; Isa. 54:17).

Yours is the Kingdom and the power and the glory forever. Amen.

KEY APOSTOLIC PRAYERS

Prayer for the spirit of revelation to know Him in His power. (Eph. 1:17–21)

I keep asking that the God of our Lord Jesus Christ, the glorious Father, may give you the Spirit of wisdom and revelation, so that you may know him better. I pray that the eyes of your heart may be enlightened in order that you may know the hope to which he has called you, the riches of his glorious inheritance in his holy people, and his incomparably great power for us who believe. That power is the same as the mighty strength he exerted when he raised Christ from the dead and seated him at his right hand in the heavenly realms, far above all rule and authority, power and dominion, and every name that is invoked, not only in the present age but also in the one to come.

Prayer for the release of supernatural strength in the heart to know Him in His fullness. (Eph. 3:16–19)

> I pray that out of his glorious riches he may strengthen you with power through his Spirit in your inner being, so that Christ may dwell in your hearts through faith. And I pray that you, being rooted and established in love, may have power, together with all the Lord's holy people, to grasp how wide and long and high and deep is the love of Christ, and to know this love that surpasses knowledge—that you may be filled to the measure of all the fullness of God.

Prayer for God's love to abound and bear fruit to His glory. (Phil. 1:9–11)

> And this is my prayer: that your love may abound more and more in knowledge and depth of insight, so that you may be able to discern what is best and may be pure and blameless for the day of Christ, filled with the fruit of righteousness that comes through Jesus Christ—to the glory and praise of God.

Prayer to know God's will, to be faithful in ministry, and to be strengthened by intimacy with God. (Col. 1:9–12)

For this reason, since the day we heard about you, we have not stopped praying for you. We continually ask God to fill you with the knowledge of his will through all the wisdom and understanding that the Spirit gives, so that you may live a life worthy of the Lord and please him in every way: bearing fruit in every good work, growing in the knowledge of God, being strengthened with all power according to his glorious might so that you may have great endurance and patience, [12] and giving joyful thanks to the Father, who has qualified you to share in the inheritance of his holy people in the kingdom of light.

Prayer for unity within the Church across the city. (Rom. 15:5–6)

May the God who gives endurance and encouragement give you the same attitude of mind toward each other that Christ Jesus had, so that with one mind and one voice you may glorify the God and Father of our Lord Jesus Christ.

Prayer to be filled with supernatural joy, peace, and hope. (Rom. 15:13)

May the God of hope fill you with all joy and peace as you trust in him, so that you may overflow with hope by the power of the Holy Spirit.

Prayer for Israel to be saved through Jesus. (Rom. 10:1)

Brothers and sisters, my heart's desire and prayer to God for the Israelites is that they may be saved.

Prayer to be enriched with the supernatural gifts of the Holy Spirit leading unto righteousness. (1 Cor. 1:4–8)

I always thank my God for you because of his grace given you in Christ Jesus. For in him you have been enriched in every way—with all kinds of speech and with all knowledge—God thus confirming our testimony about Christ among you. Therefore you do not lack any spiritual gift as you eagerly wait for our Lord Jesus Christ to be revealed. He will also keep you firm to the end, so that you will be blameless on the day of our Lord Jesus Christ.

Prayer for the release of Apostolic ministry and to abound in love and holiness. (1 Thess. 3:9–13)

How can we thank God enough for you in return for all the joy we have in the presence of our God because of you? Night and day we pray most earnestly that we may see you again and supply what is lacking in your faith. Now may our God and Father himself and our Lord Jesus clear the way for us to come to you.

May the Lord make your love increase and overflow for each other and for everyone else, just as ours does for you. May He strengthen your hearts so that you will be blameless and holy in the presence of our God and Father when our Lord Jesus comes with all his holy ones.

Prayer to be equipped and prepared to receive the fullness of God's destiny for the church. (2 Thess. 1:11–12)

With this in mind, we constantly pray for you, that our God may make you worthy of His calling, and that by his power He may bring to fruition your every desire for goodness and your every deed prompted by faith. We pray this so that the name of our Lord Jesus may be glorified in you, and you in him, according to the grace of our God and the Lord Jesus Christ.

Prayer for the Word to be released to do its work by the power of the Holy Spirit. (2 Thess. 3:1–2)

As for other matters, brothers and sisters, pray for us that the message of the Lord may spread rapidly and be honored, just as it was with you. And pray that we may be delivered from wicked and evil people, for not everyone has faith.

Prayer for impartation of Holy Spirit boldness through the release of signs and wonders. (Acts 4:24–31)

> When they heard this, they raised their voices together in prayer to God. "Sovereign Lord," they said, "you made the heavens and the earth and the sea, and everything in them. You spoke by the Holy Spirit through the mouth of your servant, our father David: 'Why do the nations rage and the peoples plot in vain? The kings of the earth rise up and the rulers band together against the Lord and against His anointed one.' Indeed Herod and Pontius Pilate met together with the Gentiles and the people of Israel in this city to conspire against your holy servant Jesus, whom you anointed. They did what your power and will had decided beforehand should happen. Now, Lord, consider their threats and enable your servants to speak your word with great boldness. Stretch out your hand to heal and perform signs and wonders through the name of your holy servant Jesus." After they prayed, the place where they were meeting was shaken. And they were all filled with the Holy Spirit and spoke the word of God boldly.

Prayer for the release of health and prosperity. (3 John 1:2)

> Dear friend, I pray that you may enjoy good health and that all may go well with you, even as your soul is getting along well.

Prayer that we would speak boldly. (Eph. 6:19–20)

Pray also for me, that whenever I speak, words may be given me so that I will fearlessly make known the mystery of the Gospel, for which I am an ambassador in chains. Pray that I may declare it fearlessly, as I should.

RECOMMENDED READING

Myles Monroe, *Understanding the Purpose and Power of Prayer*

Mike Servello, *God's Shield of Protection*

Barbara Yoder, *The Breaker Anointing*

Graham Cooke, *Crafted Prayer*

Johnny Enlow, *The Seven Mountain Prophecy*

Dr. George Meyers, *Kingdom Business Leadership*

Jason Benedict, *Blessed2Bless*

Jerry L. Williamson, *The Pulse of a Nation*

Kevin J. Conner, *The Church in the New Testament*

ABOUT THE AUTHOR

CRAIG KUEHN serves as Vice President of the Ministries Division for Go To Nations. He works with executive, regional, national, and local leaders to establish healthy field teams and to advance ministry around the globe. The Ministries Division represents more than nine hundred missionaries, affiliates, national workers, and staff operating in nearly one hundred nations on five continents. Craig and his wife, Sandra, have been married for over forty-two years. They began serving as Regional Directors for Asia in 1994. They pioneered a ministry training movement that has seen more than fifty-six hundred trained workers in more than one hundred locations, in a dozen nations, and some of the least reached nations in the world. Craig is a champion of spiritual fathers as apostolic leaders, building a team as an apostolic family, generational ministry, contending for the "full rights" of sonship and the Matthew 28 mandate to make disciples of all nations.